Organizing Wonder

Seven-year-old Terra has diagrammed her observations
in an investigation of which ball bounces the highest.

Organizing Wonder

Making Inquiry Science Work in the Elementary School

JODY S. HALL

with
Carol Callahan
Helen Kitchel
Patricia Pierce
Pedie O'Brien

HEINEMANN
Portsmouth, NH

To
Pat Pierce
teacher, colleague, friend

Heinemann
A division of Reed Elsevier Inc.
361 Hanover Street
Portsmouth, NH 03801–3912
http://www.heinemann.com

Offices and agents throughout the world

© 1998 by Joanna S. Hall

Library of Congress Cataloging-in-Publication Data
Hall, Joanna S.
    Organizing wonder : making inquiry science work in the elementary
school / Joanna S. Hall with Carol Callahan . . . [et al.].
        p.   cm.
    Includes bibliographical references (p. 107).
    ISBN 0-325-00045-X (alk. paper)
    1. Science—Study and teaching (Elementary)—United States.
I. Title.
LB1585.3.H35   1998
372.3'5'044—dc21   98-10306
                                                           CIP

Editor: William Varner
Production: Elizabeth Valway
Cover design: Darci Mehall
Manufacturing: Louise Richardson

Printed in the United States of America on acid-free paper
02   01   00   DA   2   3   4   5

Contents

Foreword by Wynne Harlen
vii

Preface
ix

Acknowledgments
xi

Introduction
xiii

Part 1: Overview

One
Theory Matters in Elementary Science
1

Two
Children as Scientists
Past and Present
13

Three
Organizing Wonder
26

Four
Teachers Talking to Teachers
Issues in Getting Started
43

Part 2: Teachers' Reflections

Five
What's in a Wave?
Carol Callahan
52

Six
Balls in Motion
We Could Make History with This!
Helen Kitchel
66

Seven
Learning About Light
Pedie O'Brien
83

Eight
Moving from Exploration to Investigation
Pat Pierce
95

Epilogue
103

References
107

Foreword

Having been party to the work in which this book originated, I am very pleased to have been asked to write a foreword. The book draws on events that took place in the 1980s and 1990s and sets them in the context, both historically and theoretically, of developments in elementary school science. In doing so it addresses issues and reflects values that are enduring ones and that are ever associated with teaching science to children.

Learning science, if there is to be understanding and not just parroting of facts, is a complex matter. It involves using mental and manipulative skills to try to make sense of things that are observed in the world around us. These "things" may be objects, events, or changes, and "making sense" means fitting them into our developing understanding of similar things. Learning science means questioning what is observed, trying to explain (developing hypotheses about) what is going on, finding answers to questions, and testing hypotheses. In science, questions are answered and hypotheses are tested by collecting evidence, either through direct investigation and experiment or by using evidence gained by others. The careful gathering and interpretation of evidence and its use in answering the original question or testing the ideas behind the hypothesis can lead to the development of understanding. Clearly, both scientific process skills and ideas are involved here, intertwined and hardly separable except for the convenience of identifying them as important goals.

Beyond this theoretical statement about the development of understanding in science, there is so much more to bringing about this learning with children in practice. Teachers must help children ask the kinds of questions that can be answered by investigation; encourage children to express their ideas (hypotheses); and help children collect useful evidence, interpret it, link new experiences with previous ones, and develop ideas that are consistent with the evidence. There are several key factors in providing this help: time, talk, materials, and sources of information. That it takes a great deal of time for children to explore materials or events before they are able to investigate them more systematically is something well illustrated in the chapters of *Organizing Wonder*. So, too, is the value of talk. This cannot be overemphasized, for not only do talk and discussion enable ideas and experiences to be shared, but they enable the learners to reflect upon their own understanding.

But it is not only children who benefit from time to reflect and talk through ideas. This whole book is a description of the value to teachers of having time to discuss their ideas about teaching, and it is an example of what can emerge from communicating ideas, both in writing as well as in discussion. Jody Hall distills from this experience a series of steps that marks out a path through the complexity of teaching. These set out the child-centered approach to education on which the book is founded in the kind of detail that other teachers will find most helpful, particularly when starting investigative science in their classrooms. Later, they will want to adapt the approach to meet the needs of different children in different circumstances.

Jody Hall introduces as a theme in the discussion the notion of comparing children's initial ideas about the natural world to their first drafts in writing. The basis for redrafting is, of course, different in science than in writing, but the analogy is helpful, particularly in underlining the importance of respecting children's ideas, however odd they may seem, and in taking them as the starting point for modification and development. It also helps us to remember that thinking as well as doing is central to helping children to change their ideas toward ones that are more widely applicable and closer to the accepted scientific view. There should be no conflict between the "right" answer and what children conclude from their investigations, for what is "right" is what fits the evidence obtained, providing this has been obtained in a fair way and relevant observations have been made. Often this will not be the case with young children, which is the reason why the development of the skills of collecting, selecting, and interpreting information has to be a central aim of science education. It is by working toward this aim that we help children achieve scientific understanding.

Wynne Harlen

Preface

One summer afternoon John, my son, wanted to start a fire with a magnifying glass. He chose a piece of thick watercolor paper and took it outside with a magnifying glass. He held the magnifier at random angles and heights for not much more than a minute. "Hey," he said to me, "this looks like bumpy mountains." Switching gears, he then dropped the magnifier onto the grass and headed to the swing. Brief as this episode was, John, at age seven, learned two things. He saw that paper is more than what first meets the eye: this kind of paper had a "bumpy" surface. He also found out that magnified light directed for a short time on paper does not produce very much heat. In the right conditions, he might extend his learning about the many properties of paper and light by exploring with the guidance of a knowledgeable adult.

How can teachers cultivate wonder? How can we hold children's attention, foster their questions, and expand their understanding of the natural world? These are the questions that have shaped my work with colleagues since 1988. They arise in the context of national, state, and local attempts to set standards in the subject areas. Teachers need approaches to learning and teaching in science that are aligned with *Benchmarks for Scientific Literacy* (American Association for the Advancement of Science 1993), *National Science Education Standards* (National Research Council 1996), and the various state standards in science.

Organizing Wonder is about an inquiry approach to the study of the natural world. Children work directly with materials as young "scientists," raising questions and answering them in explorations and investigations. The approach takes as its starting point children's ideas and the challenge to deepen those ideas. This book is the work of a group of second- through fifth-grade elementary teachers and myself—an educator working at the college level who wanted to find an approach to learning and teaching in science comparable to new literacy practices. At the outset of our work together we worked intensively with Dr. Wynne Harlen of the Scottish Council for Research in Education, a world leader in the field of elementary science education. Because of this association, we were able to draw from several versions of the English national curriculum in science (Department of Education and Science 1988, 1989, and 1991; Department for Education and Employment 1995). These documents are comparable to state and national standards developed somewhat later in the United

States in the 1990s, having drawn heavily from the same research
into the development of children's thinking about the natural world.
Harlen was a member of the original task force that set out the English standards. In our work with children we combined the learning
goals of developmental standards with the approach Harlen set out in
Primary Science: Taking the Plunge (1985a) and in *Developing Science in the
Primary Classroom* (1990).

The teachers and I have had extensive experience in developing
the approach advanced in *Organizing Wonder*. In July of 1987 we participated in a summer institute in which Dr. Harlen introduced us to
her research and practical experience in this field. In the year that followed, supported by Harlen, the teachers and I met in follow-up
workshops, and the teachers conducted case studies in their schoolrooms. This led to the formulation of questions about organizing and
sustaining wonder. Over the next five years the teachers and I worked
together doing action research in a curriculum study group.

A premise of *Organizing Wonder* is that elementary teachers can
orchestrate inquiry science without having to depend on step-by-step
manuals, in much the same way as we conduct a writing workshop
approach. To do so, however, a teacher needs to have a framework in
mind for generating children's ideas and questions—a framework for
planning inquiry that leads to the fair testing of ideas about the natural world. *Organizing Wonder* maps out such an approach. The book
begins with an overview section (Chapters 1–4) describing the theory
and research behind the practice, historical antecedents, a step-by-
step explanation of the approach, and issues facing teachers who start
to teach in this way. In the next section (Chapters 5–8), four teachers
reflect on their practice. The writing styles vary: some parts are theoretical and some are practical; one is a transcription of teachers talking
to teachers; and one is a narrative account of the work of the group.

We have written *Organizing Wonder* because we wanted to share
our experiences with a standards-based approach that takes as its
starting point children's ideas. This project has provided us with the
rare opportunity, in the field of education, of fine-tuning an approach
in a highly focused, pragmatic way for several years. *Organizing Wonder*
appears at a point when elementary teachers are asking themselves,
How can we address the new science standards in our teaching? In
reading *Organizing Wonder*, you may substitute your own state or local
standards for the American and English national standards; they stem
from the same research base.

We wish you well in your efforts to learn with children about the
natural world. We have found that the enthusiasm and excitement
accompanying the exploration and investigation of the things of this
world bring deep pleasure to the art of teaching.

Acknowledgments

I have served in several capacities: coordinator of the institute and follow-up workshops, instructor for case study work, coordinator for the curriculum group, and collaborator with individual teachers in working with children in schoolroom settings. The two districts from which the teachers come, Addison Central and Addison Northeast Supervisory Unions in Vermont, contributed release time and allocated Title II funds to the project. I received support from the Barker Foundation, Fulbright Commission, Middlebury College, and Pine Manor College. Many people contributed their support to this project in its various phases. Lisa Beck, a primary teacher and colleague, has been a particularly important contributor. As an integral member of our group for three years, she helped to fine-tune the approach presented in *Organizing Wonder*. Her perspective is particularly evident in Chapter 4. We would also like to thank Mia Allen, Nina Bacon, Lynne Balman, Phoebe Barash, Bonnie Bourne, Stan Chu, Dick Dollase, Hu Dyasi, Bob Gleason, Addison Hall, David Hamilton, Wynne Harlen, Linda Horowitz, Gregg Humphrey, Sue Lewis, Sue Liberty, Jim Lombardo, Alan Myers, Tom Popkewitz, Bob Prigo, Dan Rubenstein, Carol Sampson, Henry Scipione, Connie Skinger, Kathleen Tosiello, and Ron Wastnedge. We are grateful for their assistance.

We wish to dedicate this book to Pat Pierce, who died of cancer in 1994. For *Organizing Wonder* she wrote about her work with forces. She had planned another chapter about her pond work, in particular about her fourth- and fifth-graders' investigation of the link between how canivores and herbivores are built and what they do. Pat's enthusiasm for the adventure of learning with children and colleagues was contagious! She thrived on twenty or so children immersed in a steady flow of revelations about the natural world. Where there was action, Pat was in the thick of it! And there is plenty of action in an inquiry approach.

Introduction

In the mid-eighties I began to ask, What is science in the elementary school? Or, put another way, What might it be? What kinds of educational experiences do teachers and teacher-educators need to teach science? On one level I was searching for ways of working with elementary children and ways of supporting teachers in learning new practices. At a deeper level, I was looking for a specific kind of approach analogous to the process approach to writing.

Several teachers in my area shared my interest. In the field of writing, all of us had come to value our own life experience as the basis of writing and set up our classrooms as writing workshops—a practice that continues to this day. We had learned to make students' ideas and experiences a starting point in writing by participating in writing workshops and reading the work of Peter Elbow, Donald Graves, and James Moffett, and later of Nancie Atwell and Lucy Calkins. Students start with inchoate thought and begin to shape it through writing. They learn about the conventions of different kinds of writing through reading and learn to use them in their own writing. With this in mind we asked ourselves, Can we make students' ideas and experiences a starting point in studying the natural world?

In the area of reading, we had come to value high-quality children's literature as a primary motivating factor in engaging our students in print. Our schoolrooms were places where students had easy access to lots of books. We had learned new ways of structuring reading activities to get at the meaning of texts, and we no longer had to depend on the step-by-step instructions of basal manuals. Now we asked, How can we bring into the schoolroom the materials, events, and living things of the natural world, and the equipment to explore them?

These questions led me to the work of English science educator Wynne Harlen, whom I met in 1985. Her answer to my questions indicated that I had found someone who could help us:

> Children need help to criticize their own ideas. It's hard to shake such ideas as the notion that light comes from the eyes. Children can be given opportunities to think about light in lots of different ways in order to change the ideas of light that are formed in everyday life. [Interview 1985]

This sounded a lot like drafting, revising, and editing a piece of writing. She briefly described a range of activities children could carry out. In 1987 I made arrangements for Harlen and her colleague, English science educator Sheila Jelly—author of the *schools council's, Minibeasts* (1974), and co-author with Harlen of *Developing Science in the Primary Classroom* (1990), to lead a summer institute for educators in Vermont.

The summer institute gave me and thirty-one other educators a starting point for answering our questions. In the year following the institute, I orchestrated a first round of follow-up work with release time for teachers to reflect on implementation and to experience further guidance from Hubert Dyasi and Stanley Chu of the Workshop Center at City College of New York. In addition, I worked with twelve teachers who did an action-research project on children's use of science process skills. Throughout that first year we struggled to determine how to use children's questions and ideas as starting points and how to orchestrate what follows. It seemed like a promising tunnel, with light glimmering faintly ahead.

Fixed in my mind was the vision of getting children to write several drafts out of their own ideas. The model for learning and teaching in science provided by Harlen, Jelly, Elstgeest, and Osborne in *Primary Science* (Harlen 1985a) encouraged us to believe that we could get children to raise questions and hypotheses for investigation, but we found this much harder to do in reality. In that first year much of our work was sketchy, rarely extended beyond one day, and involved little fair testing. At that point we were focused on getting some kind of science activity going in the classroom—anything—and assessing students' process skills of observing, hypothesizing, raising questions, predicting, communicating, and investigating. For the most part we were unable to recognize hypotheses and questions in the children's work, much less provide opportunities for investigations that grew out of them. In one classroom, over a two-week period, children explored water dropping on different surfaces, observed what floats and what sinks, and made clay boats. In another, children planted bean seeds, explored plastic pipe fittings, and floated clay boats. Activities were staged as one-day-only experiences; for the most part the activity that followed was another kind of science topic marginally related to what came before. Exciting as these activities were, children did not have much of an opportunity to become aware of their thinking in any one area or to control it.

The story of one teacher early in our first year together shows how we were struggling to find in children's ideas the seeds for future work, and how we began to see a way out of our quandary. Carol Callahan was determined to try to find some clues for extending science activity on the basis of children's ideas. She had set the children to work by posing the question, "Does the surface affect the size and shape of the drops of water?" The children worked enthusiastically, though they had other interests. Carol noted:

> Kate and Ben became intrigued with how they could see the table through wet paper. They noticed that their math paper seemed to be of the same kind of paper as newsprint. It was easier to see the table through the math paper, because the print got in the way on the newspaper.

> Roger and John timed how long it took different material to absorb water. They timed by counting. They recorded this on paper.

The children's attention to issues unrelated to her question did not upset Carol, who was always open to free exploration. She was pleased with their enthusiasm and impressed by their observations, but she was uncertain about how to provide further opportunities based on their responses in this session. She asked me to come to her schoolroom so that we could figure out what to do next.

Carol and I looked over the children's responses. What she had for evidence was her sketchy notes taken while students were working and their brief written observations. I noted the wide range of observations and found out from Carol that the whole class had not discussed their observations. Based on the wide range of interests expressed, it seemed to me that a whole-class discussion of observations would help students focus their thinking and build up a direction for further work. Among the observations we noticed several dealing with the magnification properties of water. Perhaps, we agreed, further work should grow in that direction.

Together we planned the next session. Carol would start with a discussion in which students could share their observations and ideas. She also decided to pursue their interest in magnification by ending the session with an exploration of water drops on plastic wrap. Later, Carol described the discussion:

> We talked about size, shape, and absorption. The children discussed far more in these three areas than they had recorded on paper and far more than what I had perceived myself! One of the students noticed very fine details that are relevant and described a sequence of events. She drew on the chalkboard the beginning shape of a drop of water soaking into construction paper, and then described how the water was absorbed and became a circle on the paper.

Overall, Carol was ecstatic about the children's ability to verbalize so many important observations from hands-on work. Previously she had not given children much time for discussion. She noticed a tremendous difference between what they had recorded and what they were able to discuss. In the future, she said, she wanted her children to "talk, talk, talk"!

She followed up on their interest in magnification by giving them plastic wrap, water, and droppers, and by inviting them to "see what happens when you look at drops of water on plastic wrap." This led, in another session, to the children's constructing plastic-wrap-and-water magnifiers. This was one of the first times we successfully linked activities that followed children's ideas and questions.

At the same time, Pedie O'Brien expressed a need for more structure in our approach. My work with Carol and the evidence from the action-research project indicated that most teachers did a topic for a day and then switched to another; that teachers for the most part were unable to identify children's ideas and questions; and that most were far from doing any kind of fair testing. I began to realize that it would take much longer than I had anticipated to achieve something approximating the vision set out in *Primary Science*.

After reviewing the work of the first year, I concluded that the teachers and I should work on doing several related explorations as a way of building up children's ideas on a topic. At the same time, we would be on the look-out for hypotheses that could be fair tested by controlling variables. Wynne Harlen provided us with the 1988 draft of the English national curriculum; we used it as a reference, seeking to support the growth and development of children's understanding of scientific concepts. This was the point at which we began to structure our work around standards.

The most important outcome of the first year, it seems to me, was the new emphasis we began to attach to the phase of exploration. We came to realize that budding young scientists and their teachers begin in this phase to slip into a fuller awareness of the multiple variables that operate in any given science topic. That fuller awareness cannot be rushed. It takes time and several exposures. Until there is a high buildup of knowledge of the variables, it is not possible to move forward to fair testing and controlling them.

Carol Callahan, Helen Kitchel, Pedie O'Brien, Pat Pierce, and I—along with first-grade teacher Lisa Beck and sixth-grade teacher Mia Allen—formed a curriculum study group to pilot the two-phase approach of several explorations leading to investigation. Over the next six years we worked on and off, fine-tuning this approach with children and collecting materials for this book. In the first three years the group concentrated on extending explorations. The school districts provided five release-time days in the first year so that we could meet to do hands-on work ourselves and to plan our next steps. I spent considerable time working with teachers and children in schoolrooms. We learned to craft exploration questions, to conduct discussions, to identify student questions and ideas, to relate them to standards, and to extend explorations that grow out of children's ideas.

In this period I took a sabbatical year to work on this manuscript and on my doctoral thesis. When we submitted a draft to the publisher, the readers pointed out that we needed more evidence of schoolroom work, especially of the development from exploration to investigation. We had to admit they had a case. My coauthors and I went on to conduct further rounds of exploration leading to investigation, slowed by the challenge of needing to plan and execute the intensive work of sustained science. As time went on, we became even more expert in the two-stage approach. With time, you will be, too.

Chapter One

Theory Matters in Elementary Science

Two six-year-old children are working together. One angles a mirror toward the ceiling. The other points a flashlight at the mirror and waves it back and forth. They watch the reflections dancing on the ceiling.

These children are exploring the properties of light. Their teacher and I circulate around the room making shorthand observations about their activity. We are on the lookout for what interests them—for their ideas about and observations of light. The teacher and I are able to work closely together because we share a common set of beliefs about learning and teaching elementary science, which are summed up as follows:

> The aim of inquiry science is for children to develop their ideas about the natural world. Understanding grows as children work collaboratively with each other, with the teacher, and with materials, in situations structured to contribute to their ideas or hypotheses and their questions. Guided by the teacher, the children's hypotheses and questions lead to investigation involving the *beginnings* of fair testing—controlling variables—and to the revision of ideas in the direction of conventional scientific ideas.

Simple as this statement about teaching and learning science may seem, embedded in it is a set of meanings—theoretical positions and findings from research and practice—that circulate currently in the

1

schooling community. In order to make decisions about what kind of science to teach, it is necessary to understand the background of these positions. This chapter is mostly about the beliefs embedded in the practice.

Developmental Science Curriculums

The organization of teaching around a sequence of ideas about the natural world became a driving force behind curriculum reform in the nineties. In the area of light, for example, it is thought that young children in their first years at school can learn that light comes from different sources and that it passes through some materials and not others. Further along they can learn that light can change direction. At the end of their elementary school years they can learn that light travels in straight lines and understand how light is reflected. Hierarchical arrangements of scientific ideas have been derived from the empirical findings of researchers and the experience of practitioners. At present these hierarchies act as curriculum guidelines in a range of national and state documents on scientific literacy issued in the nineties. They are thought of as standards, benchmarks, or targets that the teacher should keep in mind while planning schoolroom activity. An analysis of the content of the American national guidelines reveals that more than 90 percent of the material to be learned is specific content or scientific ideas and the remainder is inquiry skills. The pendulum in elementary science has swung away from the sixties' and seventies' emphasis on the processes of science, such as observing and predicting. This is unlike the emphasis in mathematics and English language arts, which has swung in the other way to problem solving and process writing. The approach taken in this book is a balance between the two.

In 1983 Rosalind Driver, an English researcher who studies children's learning in science, suggested that a developmental sequence of children's ideas would aid teachers in organizing schoolroom activity. Driver justified her recommendation on three counts: studies of children's developmental ideas about natural phenomena; psychologist David Ausebel's theory that learners structure knowledge in a framework of concepts; and psychologist Jerome Bruner's proposal for a spiral curriculum. Studies of children's ideas, she said, "indicate that these develop with age through a clear sequence, and knowledge of this can be helpful both in deciding at what age to teach a topic and how to organize appropriate experiences" (Driver 1983). Although developmental sequences of concepts have been considered since the fifties, enough studies of children's thinking in science existed by the eighties that frameworks could be proposed.

The first such sequence appeared in a 1988 draft of the English/Welsh National Science Curriculum, *Science for Ages 5 to 16* (Department of Education and Science and the Welsh Office 1988). Guidelines in sixteen areas of science were laid out, as were four areas of investigation and communication skills. The hierarchies were derived from the working party's judgement, "their collective experience and knowledge of what pupils are capable of at different ages." For example, at the primary level the study of "sound" is expressed in terms of the knowledge and understanding of the subject to be learned. Levels 1 to 3 are attainment targets for children age four to seven and levels 2 to 5 are targets for children ages eight to eleven.

Level 1

- Know that sounds can be made in a variety of ways.

Level 2

- Know that sounds are heard when the sound reaches the ear.
- Be able to explain how musical sounds are produced in simple musical instruments.

Level 3

- Know that sounds are produced by vibrating objects and can travel through different materials.
- Be able to give a simple explanation of the way in which sound is generated and can travel through different materials.

Level 4

- Know that it takes time for sound to travel.

Level 5

- Understand that the frequency of a vibrating source affects the pitch of the sound it produces.
- Understand the relationship between the loudness of a sound and the amplitude of vibration of the source.
- Understand the importance of noise control in the environment.

Although these statements constitute a clear sequence, the task force, which included Driver, acknowledged that "children's learning often proceeds in an irregular way."

In the 1995 version, *The National Curriculum: Science* (Department of Education and Employment), three areas of science replace the sixteen areas of science, and one area of investigation and communication skills replace four areas. Key stage 1 replaces levels 1 to 3, and key stage 2 replaces levels 2 to 5. The area of sound is reduced to fewer attainment targets. At key stage 1 (ages four to seven), children should be taught the following.

- There are many kinds of sound and many sources of sound.
- Sounds travel away from sources, getting fainter as they do so.
- Sounds are heard when they enter the ear.

Children at key stage 2 (ages eight to eleven) should be taught the following.

- Sounds are made when objects, *e.g. strings on musical instruments,* vibrate but that vibrations are not always directly visible.
- The pitch and loudness of sounds produced by some vibrating objects, *e.g. a drum skin, a plucked string,* can be changed.
- Vibrations from sound sources can travel through a variety of materials, *e.g. metals, wood, glass, air,* to the ear.

In 1993 the American Association for the Advancement of Science (AAAS) released *Benchmarks for Scientific Literacy.* The aim of this project is to build on the AAAS publication *Science for All Americans* (1990), in which adult scientific literacy in twelve areas of science, technology, and mathematics is defined. The result is a hierarchy of antecedent ideas or benchmarks clustered according to grade level groupings: K–2; 3–5; 6–8; and 9–12. For example, the following benchmarks characterize an understanding of the motion of objects:

K–2

- Things move in many different ways, such as straight, zigzag, round and round, back and forth, and fast and slow.
- The way to change how something is moving is to give it a push or pull.
- Things that make sound vibrate.

3–5

- Something that is moving may move steadily or change its direction. The greater the force is, the greater the change in motion will be. The more massive an object is, the less effect a given force will have.
- How fast things move differs greatly. Some things are so slow that their journey takes a long time; others move too fast for people to even see them.

While the rhetoric of *Benchmarks* indicates that it is "a grassroots movement" coming from "in-the-trenches educators," it is apparent that children's concepts about the natural world laid out hierarchically are dominant. "Research on student's understanding and learning," the report states, "bears significantly on the selection and grade placement of the benchmarks." Rosalind Driver's work, in particular, is noted as influencing the work of the project. In adopting a hierarchical arrangement of concepts, the English national curriculum and *Benchmarks* have a lot in common.

The ethos of *Benchmarks* is that students are to encounter goals in the areas of mathematics, science, and technology together in many different learning situations. The report takes as a given that integrated learning promotes usage outside of school. Accordingly teachers are to combine benchmarks from these areas in their planning. In this way, it is thought, the integration of areas of knowledge and ways of investigating will result, and separation into individual science subjects will decline. In their view scientific learning is NOT the understanding of each of the separate disciplines.

The *National Science Education Standards* (1996), put out by the National Research Council (NRC), also sets out concepts that are "developmentally appropriate for students at the grade level specified." The selection of content standards was made on the basis of the centrality of each idea or principle and the richness of its explanatory power. As an example, physical science standards for position and motion of objects, for grades K–4, are expressed as follows:

- The position of an object can be described by locating it relative to another object or the background.

- An object's motion can be described by tracing and measuring its position over time.

- The position and motion of objects can be changed by pushing and pulling. The size of the change is related to the strength of the push or pull.

- Sound is produced by vibrating objects. The pitch of the sound can be varied by changing the rate of vibration.

The four developmental frameworks described above identify scientific ideas appropriate for children at different ages. All four are useful references for schoolroom practice, as are comparable state standards. We have found that they do provide a useful "ballpark" frame of reference for teachers.

Yet while these hierarchies are useful for a general orientation to what children of different ages can and can't do, there are reasons for caution. There is no clear, compelling evidence that children actually do proceed upward through an incremental hierarchy in the sequence that has been laid out. Indeed, anyone who has listened to a group of ten-year-old children discussing, for example, the forces acting on a bridge they are making, will hear a wide range of concepts expressed within the course of ten minutes. Concepts come and go like the wind in children's minds. Researchers themselves acknowledge that children's ideas are multifaceted and highly variable (Driver, Guesne, and Tiberghien 1985). These hierarchical arrangements represent the ordering of different children's ideas from a mature perspective, rather than the typical child's actual step-by-step, longitudinal acquisition of a mature scientific understanding of the natural world. In any case, the empirical studies of children's learning about the natural world are collected in the current context of the well-known low level of instruction in science (American Association for the Advancement of Science 1993). Other reasons for caution with these frameworks are their suggestion that development is a standardized set of limited understandings, that learning can be dispensed as so many piecemeal facts, and that teachers should attend only to children's ideas that match the ideas listed in any one of these reductivist hierarchies. In looking at these hierarchies for some kind of orientation, therefore, it is important to regard them as suggestive of possibilities. What the studies of children's ideas indicate is a range of ideas that children can learn.

The Tenacity of Prior Ideas About the Natural World

Research since the seventies into children's thinking about the natural world shows that they form strong ideas at an early age. These prior ideas are tenacious and prevent the understanding of more complex scientific explanations in secondary school. For example, in the content area of force and motion, Lou, a thirteen-year-old identified as gifted, provides a vivid example of how previous ideas influence school learning (Gunstone and Watts 1985). The students were asked to predict and compare the times taken for one-inch cubes of plastic and aluminum to fall about two meters. Lou answered, "The heavier [aluminum] one will get there first." When the two cubes were dropped, Lou claimed to see the aluminum cube hit the ground first. Most people present saw the two cubes hit the ground together. Lou's prior belief so strongly influenced his observation in science class that he was unable to see what everyone else witnessed.

Driver (1983) noted that students "view the world through the spectacles of their own preconceptions, and many have difficulty in making the journey from their own intuitions to the ideas presented in science lessons." Extensive interviews with children about a wide range of natural phenomena reveal their ideas. Following are conclusions reached as a result of this research that are useful for the teacher:

1. Children have views about a variety of topics in science from a young age, and prior to learning science at school.

2. Children's views are often different from scientists' views, but to children they are sensible, useful views.

3. Children's views can remain uninfluenced, or be influenced in unanticipated ways, by science teaching. (Osborne 1985)

The implication for teaching is that new approaches must help children to change their ideas. As Driver (1983) put it,

> Techniques which are being incorporated into these approaches include providing opportunities for pupils to make their own ideas explicit, encouraging the generation and testing by pupils of alternative interpretations of phenomena, and giving pupils experiences which challenge their current ideas.

This kind of trial-and-error learning is what Driver calls *constructivism*, because theories are "constructions of the human mind whose link with the world of experience comes through the processes by which they are tested and evaluated."

The question for practitioners is, What kind of trial-and-error learning can children do? Can children hypothesize? Can they learn how to fair test and control variables? These are the procedural skills that received less attention than scientific ideas in national guidelines on scientific literacy.

Trial-and-Error Learning: What Kind and to What Degree?

It is in this area that Jean Piaget's work has been so influential. Piaget's findings place limitations on the kind and degree of thinking children can do. Many who write science education textbooks, formulate policy, and contribute to curriculum frameworks accept Piaget's stage theory with little reference to challenges to these limitations. Here, for example is an excerpt from an elementary science methods textbook (Gega 1991), which explains the terms of the two Piagetian stages of childhood—the "preoperational" stage from about ages two to seven, and the "concrete operational" stage from about ages seven to twelve:

"Intuitive thought" captures well how four- to seven-year-olds think. They typically use their sense impressions or intuition rather than logic in forming judgments. They also find it hard to remember more than one thing at a time.

Concrete operational children, on the other hand, can do much logical thinking. Their handicap is that the ideas they consider must be tied to concrete materials they can manipulate. Or, at least, they must have had some firsthand experience with the materials to think about them.

The author goes on to say that the cause-and-effect thinking of children under the age of seven is inconsistent and magical. The Piagetian view holds that the egocentrism of young children under the age of seven affects their perception of objects (e.g., the sun follows them as they walk), and that children's failure to conserve number, length, amount, area, weight, and volume has a negative impact on science understanding. What they can do, we are told, is use their senses to sort living and nonliving things, one property at a time. Practitioners who subscribe to this view feature sorting as the main kind of science activity for children under the age of seven. The description of concrete operational children does not provide much guidance for teachers in terms of how much fair testing children might be able to do.

English science educator Wynne Harlen (1985b) demonstrated a Piagetian developmental view of children's reasoning in science that has greater specificity than the previous example and that indicates the possibility of more advanced work, especially for children above the age of seven. Five- to seven-year-olds "need to be able to act on things, to explore, manipulate, describe, sort and group them" (Harlen 1985b). With plenty of experience, they "replace some action by thought and they are then on the way to rational thinking." Harlen found that children from approximately the age of seven can experiment. They can raise their own questions and find answers: "They can be helped to realize that some of the questions they ask can be answered by doing more than just observing things closely." They can conduct "investigations of the effect on some object or system of changing a variable systematically, keeping other things the same." From age nine children can "to some extent handle problems which involve more than one variable." At approximately age eleven children change in the direction of "occasional speculation about hypothetical situations and abstract ideas." Some will be able to manipulate abstract ideas, use logical relations at a general level, and view situations from a variety of viewpoints. Most children up to the age of thirteen, however, will "not have these abilities, but may be taking some strides in developing them."

What is given less attention in science educators' reference to Piagetian theory and empirical findings is that Piaget's view of the limitations of children's thinking is not universally accepted. A well-known challenge to Piaget in this matter came from Scottish developmental psychologist Margaret Donaldson in *Children's Minds* (1978). After reviewing a range of studies, she concluded that children can decenter and use reason—at younger ages than Piaget found—when the intentions of experimenters are closer to children's expectations and interpretations than Piaget's had been (i.e., when situations make sense to children). Psychologist and early childhood teacher Susan Isaacs reached the same conclusion in 1930, when she challenged most of Piaget's earliest findings on the basis of her own research at the Malting House School in Cambridge, England. Donaldson and Isaacs are not alone; others believe children can perform at higher levels earlier than Piaget thought possible (Bruner 1960; Gagne 1977), but this view is given short shrift.

Another notion that constrains schoolroom practice in the area of trial-and-error learning is the notion that children can't hypothesize. The recently issued American curriculum guidelines assiduously avoid this term in describing what children under age twelve or so can and can't do in science. English science educator Wynne Harlen (1985b) argues for the more generous view that children can hypothesize, or "explain observations or relations, or [make] predictions in terms of a principle or concept." In the following passage, she justified the use of the term *hypothesize* at the elementary level:

> It describes concisely an important process in children's scientific activity which otherwise needs a clumsy phrase such as "suggesting tentative explanations". To use the word 'explaining' implies a certainty which is rarely justified. If we want children to realize that scientific knowledge is tentative and always subject to disproof or change in the light of further evidence then it is useful to introduce the word 'hypothesis' more frequently.

Here Harlen points out that the term *hypothesize* connotes the tentative nature of knowledge and relation between an idea and evidence. Even young children have ideas that they test. In the spirit of accepting beginners' efforts as sketchy "first drafts," as we have learned to do in writing and reading, it seems prudent to regard these ideas about the natural world as hypotheses to be tested.

The American schooling community is cautious about any kind of experimentation below fourth grade. The National Research Council (1996) exercised this kind of caution when it warned that students in grades K–6:

can design investigations to try things to see what happens—they tend to focus on concrete results of tests and will entertain the idea of a "fair" test (a test in which only one variable at a time is changed). However, children in K–4 have difficulty with experimentation as a process of testing ideas and the logic of using evidence to formulate explanations.

Unfortunately the Academy does not elaborate on the issue of children's use of logic. The wording "children in K–4 have difficulty with experimentation" has a dampening effect on the pursuit of investigation below the fourth-grade level. Rather than assuming that children can't hypothesize, fair test, and control variables, in the interest of raising expectations for children it seems a better strategy to create conditions in which they can make beginning efforts in these areas, much like the approximations in early literacy of invented spelling.

The American Association for the Advancement of Science (1993) specifications are even more vague about what kind of experimentation children can do. In grades K–2 it is thought that children can raise questions that can be answered by doing: "collecting, sorting, counting, drawing, taking something apart, or making something" and "making careful observations." In grades 3–5 children can conduct "investigations" (though this term is not defined), and by the end of fifth grade they should keep "records of their investigations and observations" and offer "reasons for their findings and consider reasons suggested by others." Hypothesizing with reference to evidence is reserved for grades 6–8.

In the past, when schoolrooms were organized traditionally for recitation or progressively for individual assignments or projects, the likelihood of children generating hypotheses and fair tests was low. Today, however, the schooling community encourages high-order thinking in social situations. It is within an organized social context that children begin to think and act like scientists.

Social Learning

A consensus among academic and schooling communities has emerged that the beginnings of thought exist in social interaction. Psychologist Lev Vygotsky (1978) developed the theory that thinking has a basis in social interaction and later is internalized:

> Every function in the child's cultural development appears twice, on two levels. First on the social, and later on the psychological level; first, between people as an interpsychological category, and then inside the child, as an intrapsychological category. This applies equally

to voluntary attention, to logical memory and to the formation of concepts. The actual relations between human individuals underlie all the higher functions.

Working with the teacher as a model and with other children, children can make observations of relevant details in studying the natural world, making connections and forming ideas.

As anthropologist Clifford Geertz (1973) put it, "Human thought is consummately social: social in its origins, social in its functions, social in its form, social in its applications." Children benefit from collaboratively exploring the natural world in hands-on ways, talking about observations while they work, discussing them in small groups and as a whole group, and planning and carrying out investigations in small groups. In a rationale for collaborative learning, English professor Kenneth Bruffee (1992) wrote,

> To think well as individuals we must learn to think well collectively—that is, we must learn to converse well. The first steps to learning to think better, therefore, are learning to converse better and learning to establish and maintain the sorts of social context, the sorts of community life, that foster the sorts of conversation members of community value.

Children can learn to "converse better" in the conventions of science. The teachers know what sorts of conversation the community values through reference to the curriculum guidelines, and they guide the conversations in that direction. After several explorations the children have the language skills and knowledge of the material to work together as a group to plan investigations.

Conclusion

The chapter's opening statement about the kind of science advocated in this book reads:

> The aim of inquiry science is for children to develop their ideas about the natural world. Understanding grows as children work collaboratively with each other, with the teacher, and with materials, in situations structured to contribute their ideas or hypotheses and their questions. Guided by the teacher, the children's hypotheses and questions lead to investigation involving the beginnings of fair testing—controlling variables—and to the revision of ideas in the direction of conventional scientific ideas.

Where in this statement is the wonder that sparks investigation? It must be admitted that this theoretical statement about learning in science strips the process of the glimmers of curiosity that accompany children's musings. But to orchestrate science activity, a teacher must have some theories about what is happening and why. A teacher's beliefs about children's learning in science—of hierarchies of scientific ideas, of the tenacity of prior knowledge, of the possibilities of trial-and-error learning in a social context—shape practice.

This chapter opened with a description of two six-year-old children who are exploring reflections from a flashlight. In planning an exploration of light the teacher and I drew from the theoretical frameworks discussed in this chapter. We consulted developmental science curriculum standards to get a ballpark idea of children's growing notions of light. We checked reference material that provided an intelligible scientific explanation to the nonscientist adult to make sure *we* had a clear understanding of the concepts before we began to work. Then, in view of our knowledge of the existence and tenacity of children's prior ideas, we took notes on what children said and did while working with materials to help us understand what their thinking was at the outset, before they moved o n to more advanced work. We took note of what's shown in their journals (though we do find that children's ability to express their thinking in writing is limited by the time and effort it takes to put those ideas down on paper). Next, while observing children working with materials, we focused on finding out what was hooking their interest and activity, trying to find in their ideas and observations statements that could be made over to hypotheses for investigations, and registering changes in their thinking. Finally, we involved the children in a lot of group work. We solicited children's ideas about the topic in discussions. We organized them into small groups to explore and investigate, and we took time after hands-on work to discuss developing ideas. The next chapter compares this approach to approaches taken in the past.

Chapter Two

Children as Scientists
Past and Present

Over the course of the twentieth century, the elementary schooling community has struggled to define science for children. The view taken in this book—that children benefit from inquiry science leading to conceptual change—is related to the *discovery* approaches of the sixties. At that time "discovery" connoted the use of concrete materials and children's active involvement in learning. Then, in the seventies and eighties, the focus shifted to children's use of the process skills of science (e.g., observation), and in the nineties it shifted to children's acquisition of concepts. The approach taken in this book seeks a balance in the learning and teaching of skills and concepts.

Our approach has its historical beginnings in the world of English progressive schooling. That is particularly the case in regard to its most distinctive features, including the centrality of children's questions, children's ability to state hypotheses, investigation that moves in the direction of fair testing, and faith in teachers' ability to lead investigation. This is not to say that some current American endeavors do not share these values to some degree. Certainly the recent national and state frameworks move nominally in this direction. Nor is it to claim that this approach is widely practiced in English schools today. Indeed, the situation is quite the reverse, not only because the approach is challenging and requires commitment and resources, but also because of political and economic forces that are beyond the scope of this book. The kind of inquiry science described herein is closely aligned with the work of British primary science educator Dr. Wynne Harlen, who advised me and the teachers. Dr. Harlen has been involved with science projects from the sixties into the present.

This chapter traces the beginnings of this approach in its English setting before Harlen's involvement, and compares its current status with its origins and with American elementary science approaches of the same period. A comparative, historical analysis sheds light on shifting values in practice, reveals the beginnings of standards, and helps to inform decisions about what to do when studying the natural world with children. As such, historical analysis provides teachers and other decision makers with useful language in arguing for particular practices.

Deliberations over curriculum and instruction have centered around questions of processes and concepts: What does it mean to think scientifically and to what degree can children do it? What content should be covered in the curriculum? What is the role of the teacher in addressing processes and concepts? Science projects of the sixties in the post-Sputnik era received generous support for addressing these questions. At that time dynamic teams of educators assembled to address the challenge of reform in science education.

First to be considered are two English contributions, the Nuffield Junior Science Project (NJSP) and the Oxford Primary Science Project. These two projects emanated from ongoing school reform efforts in England, with beginnings in the progressive movement at the turn of the century.

Children's Questions

> It is certainly true that children will ask many questions [though] many are of fleeting interest and require only a brief, almost casual answer. But there are times when a situation captivates a child. He will look, listen, and if possible manipulate . . . and in many cases will ask a question not always posed in the interrogative, but often expressed as a statement of belief. (Nuffield Foundation 1967a).

What is most noteworthy about the Nuffield Junior Science Project—and what links it so closely to the approach taken in this book—is a belief in children's ability to ask investigation questions, given the right conditions. In 1967 the Nuffield Foundation Science Teaching Project reported on the work of science educators and teachers in English primary schoolrooms from 1964 to 1966.

According to *Guide 1* (1967a), one of several books emanating from the project, children were to question the environment, seek answers, and gain understanding, with guidance from the teacher. It was suggested that science is a way of working that goes on in stages:

1. The teacher's first duty is to present the child with a range of materials and place him in situations which give him extensive practical sensory experience.

2. Once the children are interested in and handling things and reacting to their experiences, it is imperative for the teacher to discuss with them these reactions and the ideas they are forming.

3. . . . When the teacher and children discuss their experiences, it frequently happens that problems are raised. The child may formulate a question himself, interrogatively or as a statement of belief. . . . However his problem arises, there will be more discussion, first to help the child frame the question in such a way that a solution can be found, and secondly to decide exactly how the solution shall be sought—by experiment, from books, by asking a local expert, and so on.

4. As a result of these discussions the teacher will need to anticipate the general lines of investigation which may arise, and prepare accordingly. He should ask himself what kinds of materials should be available for the children to work with, and what books should be in class for further reading and for reference.

5. . . . When the children have carried out their investigation, there will be more discussion about their findings and what these mean.

6. The next stage will be to consider with the children how their findings may possibly be recorded and communicated and which of the possible ways would be most appropriate.

In the simplest terms, this sequence was one of extensive practical experience, discussion of ideas, question raising, experimentation, discussion of findings, and communication, though *experimentation* was not defined in terms of what children might be able to do. It was emphasized that most of science in primary school consisted of observations and the discussion of observations. "Experimentation may come," *Guide 1* stated, "but is not essential." Although project materials avoid a direct explanation of experimenting, the guides show teachers and children doing it:

> Anne P. and Gillian noticed that some birds would land fearlessly on the bird tables, while others were shy and remained on the ground under the bushes. They wondered if the colour of a table had anything to do with it, and attempted to find out whether birds were attracted by some colours and put off by others. They made four similar bird cakes and put one in each of four differently coloured plastic bowls, and then stood them on the soil in the garden. The girls expected that the birds would feed most readily out of the green

bowl because it was a similar colour to grass, but they found that the starlings and sparrows ate from all the bowls. The teacher discussed the experiment with them and they saw that it was inconclusive. They were determined to try a different one which had occurred to them as they watched the tits feeding. They drove five posts into the ground in the garden, stretched a string along the row, and hung bird cakes from it on pieces of coloured string. (Nuffield Foundation 1967a)

Anne and Gillian's question about what draws birds to feeding areas led to an experiment. The teacher's guidance helped the girls to redirect their investigation when it wasn't working out.

In highlighting children's questioning and their pursuit of interests in the environment through experimentation, the Nuffield Junior Science Project had ties to the pre–World War II pragmatic tradition of child psychologist Susan Isaacs, her coauthor husband, Nathan Isaacs (a metallurgist and educational reformer), and philosopher John Dewey. This tradition's emphasis on children's questions and its generous view of children's intellectual growth is important to the approach taken in *Organizing Wonder*. While *Guide 1* made no direct reference to that pragmatic tradition (other than a Dewey quote included in the epigraph: "Children are people. They grow into tomorrow only as they live today"), the connection came from participating teachers schooled in that tradition and from Nathan Isaacs, a consultant to NJSP (Hall 1993).

In the twenties, Susan and Nathan Isaacs had explored ways in which children ages two through eight could follow up their interests in the environment at their experimental Malting House School in Cambridge, England. They discussed their findings in *Intellectual Growth in Young Children* (1930). Susan Isaacs (1885–1948), a teacher of young children, developmental child psychologist, and psychoanalyst, brought children's encounters with the natural world into the foreground in order to take issue with the limitations Piaget placed on children's use of logic. Acting on the inspiration of John Dewey, she demonstrated how teachers could meet the spontaneous inquiries of the child. Strongly critical of Piaget's early work, she stated, "Intellectual growth certainly shows a psychological coherence, but this coherence has the elasticity and vital movement of a living process, not the rigid formality of a logical system" (Isaacs 1930).

Elsewhere in *Intellectual Growth in Young Children* she said that the complexity of children's activity in school eluded expression as a formal scheme. Instead, "children themselves compel us to look at the problem of cognition in terms of process" (Isaacs 1930). Drawing data from three and a half years of records made of everyday life at the school, Isaacs proposed that cognitive behavior was not to be thought of as a set of single unit acts of relation-finding, but as a complex dynamic series of adaptive reactions and reflections. These crystallize out here and there into clear judgements or definite hypotheses or inferences, which, however, gain all their meaning from their place in the whole movement of the child's mind in its attempt to grasp and organize its experience.

In setting out this argument, she demonstrated instances of children's learning in science. According to Isaacs, children increased their knowledge through experiences of "experiment, observation and discovery":

> One of the children had brought in a glass jar full of snow, and put it on the hot-water pipes to melt it. They kept going to look at it, and when it was melted said, "What a little bit of water it has made." Priscilla and Tommy tried to burn fragments of wool and cotton in the Bunsen flame, holding them on the point of scissors, and saying that "wool doesn't burn so easily as cotton."

In *Intellectual Growth in Young Children* Susan Isaacs demonstrated the ideas and informal structures later found in the activity and experience approach of the sixties—known in America as "open education" (Boyd and Rawson 1965; Gardner 1969; Weber 1971; Smith 1976; Simon 1991; Hall 1993). Those ideas about schooling include: learning from physical contact with the world; the value of environment, interests, and questions; complex reasoning from early childhood when interests are aroused; and the variability and versatility of children's thinking. According to Isaacs, ". . . on any day, [the children ages three to eight] would pass easily between the realms of pure phantasy and occasionally of magic, and those of practical insight and resource, and of verbal argument and reasoning."

In an appendix to *Intellectual Growth in Young Children*, Nathan Isaacs (1930) worked out his position that children's questions surge up as new situations are encountered. In the fifties and sixties, when interest in science emerged, Nathan Isaacs helped to make a case for science in the primary school, and Ron Wastnedge consulted with him before and after NJSP got off the ground. Lilian Weber (1971), a New Yorker with a lifelong interest in child-centered schooling, described her experience of a Nathan Isaacs lecture as being in the presence of "a rare mind at work, examining very deeply questions vital to education. He spoke slowly, sharing every step of his reasoning, sharing the evidence, not trying to overbear or persuade in any other way."

In the fifties and sixties Isaacs (1958) continued to promote children's questions along the lines established in "Children's 'Why' Questions." He believed that children's questions surge up when an "observation clashes with their existing scheme of thought":

Some of our chief types of finding-out questions are picked up as early as the third year; others are mastered in the fourth; and by the fifth most children are freely able to use all our main gamut. They then continually want to know: what things are—what they are made of—where they come from—how they began—what makes them happen—what makes one thing different from another—what are the reasons for apparent exceptions and anomalies, and so on.

At a 1961 British Association for the Advancement of Science conference—held to consider the place of science in the primary curriculum—it was concluded that, "It seems to be generally agreed that the approaches should be those resulting from children's questions and 'finding-out' activities" (British Association for the Advancement of Science 1962).

In 1964, at the outset of the Nuffield Junior Science Project, the team leaders made observations of teaching and learning in science in schoolrooms. According to Ron Wastnedge (1990):

Each team leader got a group of schools where the right kinds of things were happening. They dropped in on a regular basis to provide whatever help was needed. Then . . . they'd put on paper what had happened. As a result we could produce case histories for teachers to explain what it was that we were expecting them to do.

Using these observations of what was happening already in primary schools, the team developed guidelines and wrote up examples from primary teachers experienced in the tradition of Isaacs, Isaacs, and Dewey. Of 111 NJSP teachers surveyed, 35 reported that the Nuffield practices were no different from ones they had been using. "No new methods used," noted one teacher. "The idea of projects and ideas developing from the children were used in training college (1946–1948)" (Crossland 1967). Ten out of thirteen heads (primary school principals) surveyed said that Nuffield methods were already practiced in their schools.

The examples were published as a draft of *Guide 1*. The team used this publication as the main reference for more than a thousand teachers who participated in a program of trials beginning in September of 1965.

As to content, it was thought that the immediate environment—playing fields, fallen trees, and rainbow reflections—provided almost limitless opportunities. Teachers had only to alert themselves to the possibilities inherent in the environment.

The NJSP examples of children testing materials (like Anne and Gillian's study of the feeding habits of birds) made raising questions and investigating look as simple as breathing in and breathing out. While some teachers in 1967 were shown to be at ease with this kind of teaching, a government report on primary schools concluded that teachers needed more specific guidance (Schools Council 1967). Reservations notwithstanding, the examples showed that children could raise questions and investigate when the teacher knew how to guide the children in this direction. In subsequent years the government-funded Science 5/13 project picked up where NJSP left off by defining investigation in terms of objectives (Schools Council 1972) and providing further guidance for teachers.

How does NJSP compare with the model proposed in *Organizing Wonder*? Both projects emphasize the importance of children's making a lot of observations. Overall the instructional sequences of the two models are similar: Observations lead to investigation, and questions rise from children's observations. The teacher in both models provides materials and encourages the children to raise ideas for investigation. But NJSP made investigating look easy, and it did not define experimentation. In reality, inquiry science is quite likely the most challenging instructional practice to mount in elementary schooling. Complications soon arise in inquiry science unless the teacher is fully prepared to guide the children in the direction of fair testing and to more sophisticated ideas about the natural world. And that requires an understanding of the nature of fair testing and topics that can be fair tested.

Additionally, the curriculum frameworks of the nineties shed light on topics that children can investigate. Such specificity was lacking in NJSP. Furthermore, while the two approaches share a belief in children's potential for complex thought processes, NJSP ignored children's prior ideas and experiences. In recent years the science education community has come to recognize the tenacity of those ideas and the importance of bringing them into play early in the consideration of the topic.

Children and Scientific Concepts

Another English project at that time, the Oxford Primary Science Project (OPSP), was similar to NJSP in its regard for the complexity of children's thought processes. However, it structured its approach around content in the form of concepts. Because concepts play such a big role in today's definition of science for children, it is instructive to study this project's historical beginnings.

In 1964 the Ministry of Education awarded a grant to the Oxford University Institute of Education "to discover which scientific concepts could be formed by children as a result of approaches to science in the classroom and which experiences are helpful in the gradual formation of concepts" (Boyers 1965). The Oxford team, headed by Stuart Redman, took its definition of *concept* from Piagetian psychologist K. Lovell, saying "the ability of a person to discriminate or differentiate between the properties of the objects or events before him and to generalize his findings in respect of any common feature he may find." Piaget's "pioneer work" suggested to the Oxford team "a framework of smaller concepts, building up to a whole view of science" (Redman et al. 1968). Thus Piaget's highly stable mathematical concepts were remodeled into conventional concepts of science and carried into practice in the form of smaller concepts building to more complex concepts.

The Oxford team managed to skirt a critical problem that a science educator faces in drawing from Piaget: Piaget's conclusion that children are limited in their ability to think abstractly. The Oxford team argued against this limitation, in the English schooling tradition, on the basis of Susan Isaacs's research. While stating that "formal reasoning becomes significant only from the beginning of the secondary stage of education"—an observation in line with Piagetian theory, Redman et al. (1983) also noted, ". . . the child at the primary stage may be able to make abstractions about the scientific experiences which he has, and to form scientific concepts in a simple, unsophisticated form."

Citing Susan Isaacs, Redman called attention to her finding that "the thought processes of young children can be quite complicated when they are concerned with something that interests them deeply" and that children did not "always conform to the modes of thought suggested by Piaget." Accordingly, the Oxford team determined that "the child's experience must be structured in order that his understanding is gradually refined and deepened. If these concepts could be identified, it was felt that they should be investigated in the situation of the primary teacher with his class" (Redman et al. 1983).

The team decided to address the study of science in four concept areas (energy, structure, life, and chance), each with several subconcepts, in the popular form of "science that comes spontaneously from the environment of the child and his interests" (Boyers 1965). The overall approach was based on "the hypothesis that young children can be led to form scientific concepts by immersing them in 'experiences' stemming from a conceptual framework of science in the teacher's mind." In sum, OPSP combined Piaget's framework, a hierarchy of concepts in science, with elements of Susan Isaacs' pragmatic belief in children's ability to transcend Piaget's modes of thought when interests in the environment are aroused and when children are immersed in experiences leading to more sophisticated knowledge.

How does OPSP compare with the approach proposed in *Organizing Wonder*? While NJSP showed teachers and children working in the direction of fair testing and transcending Piagetian cognitive limitations, OPSP explained the theoretical and empirical basis for viewing children more generously than Piaget. The approach taken in *Organizing Wonder* shares with NJSP and OPSP the assumption that children can begin to fair test in elementary school. In that regard our approach is more in line with Susan Isaacs' pragmatic conception of schooling, or what is known today as *situated cognition*.

Messing About in Science

Another important sixties contributor to the discussion of science for children was David Hawkins, the director of the Elementary Science Study in Newton, Massachusetts, from 1962 to 1964. In 1965 Hawkins, a philosopher at the University of Colorado, participated in an NJSP workshop and established a lasting relationship with its organizer, Ron Wastnedge.

Hawkins (1965) popularized the notion of children's "messing about in science." Drawing on his work with children and teachers, he described how learning in science could be structured. Most important, "messing about" was by no means the full extent of science for children. It was but one step on the way to theorizing about experiences. He wanted children to explore before working in a more disciplined way and before thinking big thoughts about their observations. Above all, he emphasized that children shouldn't be rushed; children need to explore for a long time.

In the course of studying pendulums with children in classrooms, Hawkins hit upon a sequence of learning:

- exploratory work or "messing around"
- guidance in experimentation
- theorizing

While freely exploring materials, children gained autonomy. And, when children had gained a high degree of familiarity with pendulums, they were ready for the next step: for work that was more disciplined in the form of written and pictorial guidance. This material was to guide teachers and students in a study of pendulums—of the relations of amplitude and period. From Hawkins' point of view, teachers were unable to plan the experimentation phase; therefore experts would prepare these materials for them.

The third step was to think big thoughts about what had gone be-fore—to theorize. Theorizing worked, Hawkins said, when there ex-isted "a long build-up of latent insight, the kind of insight that the Water Rat [in *The Wind in the Willows*] had stored up from long after-noons of 'Messing About' in boats." Theorizing occurred in class dis-cussion and in lectures, and it led to the big questions about science (e.g., questions about the way different weights swing from strings of the same length). When children had enough common ground, they could sustain a serious discussion. "Theorizing in a creative sense," Hawkins said, "needs the content of experience and the logic of ex-perimentation to support it."

According to Hawkins, exploration, experimentation, and theoriz-ing in discussion were not, however, a lockstep sequence. They were often mixed and ordered in many ways, especially when new phe-nomena were observed. Hawkins' invitation for messing about in sci-ence suggested that nonscientist teachers, with the help of support materials for the investigative phase, could direct children's learning.

How does Hawkins' model compare with the approach taken in *Organizing Wonder*? Like NJSP and OPSP, Hawkins made a case for working in the direction of experimentation. What makes Hawkins distinctive—and what links him closely with our approach—is his ar-gument for intensive exploration of materials before experimentation or, in our terms, investigation. Using terms such as *messing about, don't rush*, and *a long build-up of latent insight*, Hawkins cautioned the schooling community to build up experience before experimentation and theorizing. Today, while we agree with Hawkins in the need for extensive exploration, we differ in our recognition of prior ideas and experiences that children bring to science activity. In that sense we would say, in response to Hawkins, that theorizing occurs before schoolroom activity begins, because children bring prior ideas with them to any kind of science activity. Another difference between Hawkins' approach and our view is that we believe that teachers *can* guide children in experimentation, with the help of activity books, background information about content and developing concepts, and knowledge of fair testing.

A Structure of Concepts

Other contributors to the discussion of elementary science in the six-ties thought that teachers needed even more guidance. Such is the case with the designers of the Science Curriculum Improvement Study (SCIS), which was active from the mid-sixties into the seven-ties. This project created a fixed instructional sequence for teachers to follow to help children develop a hierarchy of specific understandings about the natural world.

In the early sixties, J. Myron Atkin, a professor of education at the University of Illinois, and Robert Karplus, a professor of physics at UC Berkeley, sketched out an approach to teaching elementary science (Atkin and Karplus 1962). In their view, discovery teaching was time-consuming and inefficient. At the same time they noted the dictum of Jerome Bruner (1960) that children benefit when they discover concepts for themselves. To resolve this tension, Atkin and Karplus proposed a combination of expository and discovery teaching. Drawing from Thomas Kuhn's *The Structure of Scientific Revolutions* (1962), in which Kuhn showed how over the course of history one concept is replaced by another, Atkin and Karplus proposed that teachers introduce "modern scientific concepts" and then provide opportunities for children to "discover" those concepts in subsequent experiments. In this way children's perception was oriented in the direction of key concepts.

In 1967 Karplus, by then Director of SCIS, and Herbert Thier, Assistant Director, described the four-part learning sequence of SCIS in detail (Karplus and Thier 1967). In preliminary exploration children gained experience for later "inventions" and expressed their understanding and prior experience of the subject. Generally, this phase was a warm-up for what followed. In the conceptual invention phase, the teacher suggested "a new idea for interpreting experience, an idea which resulted from an inductive mental leap." Furnished with the new idea, children had the opportunity in the directed discovery phase to gain experience and "internalize the conceptual inventions," to "discover" a specific concept in planned situations. The final phase was analysis and the search for regularities, which might lead to repetition or further experiments and to a consideration of variables. The SCIS teacher's guides laid this sequence out in detail for the study of a hierarchy of concepts, which stretched from the observation of properties of materials in first grade to the formulation of scientific theories in sixth (i.e., in Piagetian terms, from concrete to abstract considerations). Treating teachers at the level of sous chefs, the manuals guided them with a firm hand through most steps of the way, making SCIS a good example of "teacher-proof" materials written at that time.

The approach resounded with Bruner's (1960) influential call for study in a given field, like science, to emulate the structure of that field. To begin with, the sequence bore a close resemblance to Bruner's linear processes of learning: acquisition of new information, transformation of information to make it fit new tasks, and evaluation of the adequacy of information. In matching these processes to learning in the field of science, SCIS put children in the position of beginning to act like young scientists. Furthermore, the hierarchy of increasingly complex concepts was reminiscent of Bruner's spiral curriculum, in which material was to be translated in Piagetian terms into a child's "logical forms" and built around worthy principles or concepts.

The biggest difference between SCIS and the approach taken in *Organizing Wonder* is that SCIS made very little allowance for teachers' autonomy and for children's questions and ideas. The SCIS sequence is directed to a specific concept in a situation planned by outside experts. Our approach vests in the teacher the authority to research content, to understand and direct inquiry, and to allow children's questions to lead the way to concepts. Although there was in SCIS a hierarchy of developmental concepts defined along the lines of Piagetian stages, little evidence of children's changing ideas about the natural world existed at that time.

Conclusion

In Chapter 1, we addressed current developments in science education at the elementary level:

1. research into children's ideas about the natural world
2. a view that social learning will promote greater understanding of the natural world than was thought possible in the past
3. aspirations for children to pursue their own questions and hypotheses and to deal with variables
4. frameworks of developmental curriculum in science

Looking back at the projects of the sixties from the perspective of these subsequent developments, a pattern of shifting emphases emerges. First, none of the projects took into account the presence and tenacity of children's naive ideas, and while they all made some provision for investigation, none of them defined it at Wynne Harlen's level of detail and precision. As to social learning, Hawkins and NJSP noted its value in generalized terms but provided few specifics about making it happen other than Hawkins' idea that theorizing went on in class discussion, and the NJSP suggestion that children should exchange observations after exploration and discuss the findings of their investigations. For the most part, children were to work individually: "messing about" (Hawkins), working individually at their own level in each of the four stages (SCIS), or pursing their individual interests (NJSP). In the area of developmental curriculum, SCIS and OPSP broke new ground in their attempts to define teaching and learning about the natural world in terms of "concepts"—a notion that has come to dominate the field of science education.

The principles that currently govern the practices of elementary science emanate from developmental psychology and from the constructivist movement in the field of education. Science educators such as Rosalind Driver (1983) have mapped out hierarchies of concepts. Closely linked to these hierarchies is a constructivist view of learning in science: children bring prior experiences and ideas into play when learning science, and the goal of science is advancement up a hierarchy of concepts. This view is codified in state and national curriculum frameworks.

Why has the pendulum swung in recent years to privilege hierarchies of concepts instead of investigation (or process or inquiry) skills? There is no doubt that concepts are easier to test than investigation skills. But frameworks that privilege concepts take the easy way out because it is widely accepted that inquiry skills, such as observing, questioning, and fair testing, lead to conceptual change and the kind of flexible thinking that is required to understand more and more sophisticated ideas about the natural world. An inquiry approach, however, is a challenge for teachers and students to learn. It requires professional development for teachers, fewer topics than are presently advocated in most of our new state and national standards, and time in the schoolroom. Without inquiry in science education, in a climate that privileges concepts, we run the risk of a return to rote learning. For these reasons, historical understanding of the beginnings of current standards helps members of the schooling community understand and recognize shifting relations of power and use the language of science education with greater precision in negotiations over what and how to teach.

Chapter Three

Organizing Wonder

A six-year-old boy holds a flashlight against the back side of the mirror. He is amazed: "The light won't go through!"

A girl shines a flashlight straight down on a table. The light forms a circle. She tilts the flashlight at an angle. The light forms an oval. She repeats the action several times.

Two girls stand at the doorway of the classroom. They hold pocket mirrors faceup in front of their noses. Over and over again, they approach the doorway and JUMP into the hall. One girl says, "What do you see when you get through the door?" The other says, "It looks as if you are walking on a grate, and you have to jump down."

These first- and second-grade children are fascinated by different aspects of light. Their encounters generate a sense of awe and wonder. It is unlikely, however, that these observations will lead them to a deeper level of understanding unless the teacher can guide them in firsthand work toward more sophisticated ideas about light. Why is inquiry science in which children raise questions and answer them in explorations and investigations so difficult to do with children?

Constraints on Inquiry Science that Aims for Conceptual Change

Elementary teachers understand the importance of directing student activity in science without dampening curiosity. We want to avoid placing a great deal of emphasis on lectures that go in one ear and out the other. We want to avoid whiz-bang demonstrations that seem magical and remote to students and abstracted textbook information beyond students' understanding.

Even highly directed hands-on lab experiences or work card activities seldom result in greater understanding or enjoyment of science for most elementary children. Unfortunately, these practices are the very ones most know so well from secondary school and college. Science is the hardest of all subjects to introduce at the elementary level. Restrictions operating on elementary teachers arise out of twentieth-century practices of science instruction at the secondary level and in higher education, and out of important differences between science and the mainstream subjects of the curriculum.

While elementary teachers recognize the limitations of such secondary practices as lectures, demonstrations, textbook explanations, and highly directed lab exercises, at the same time we are often uncertain about scientific ideas and about leading an inquiry into them. A teacher setting magnets down on a table, unsure of the properties of magnets and how to proceed, will find little substantive learning taking place. This predicament can lead to paralysis.

Few elementary teachers specialize in science at the college level, yet very few undergraduate preservice teachers who do study science, even as majors, plan their own investigations. Most elementary teachers have taken no more than the bare minimum of science courses. At the same time, it must be said that college courses in science, and even a degree in physics, are no guarantees that a teacher can engage eight-year-olds in the study of forces in a meaningful way.

Science has never been an important part of the elementary curriculum. Teachers have a great deal of experience in the teaching of writing, reading, and mathematics, but not science. What are the differences between science and the mainstream subjects of the elementary curriculum? To teach the conventions of text in reading we can draw from children's prior experience with the superabundance of print in our society and from the ready-made prose of skilled authors; to teach the conventions of inquiry science we can draw from children's experiences of the natural world, but then *we* are the ones who have to orchestrate materials and lead investigation. Rarely is there any other place but the schoolroom to learn about fair testing first-hand. The only way for children to learn about inquiry science is to do it with the guidance of a knowledgeable adult. In teaching writing we can rely on our own and the children's considerable knowledge of the conventions of text learned from extensive exposure to the written word, whereas few of us as teachers of science can rely on our own or the children's extensive exposure to scientific inquiry.

Swinging to another staple of the elementary curriculum, mathematics, we utilize sets of manipulatives, which often can be used to teach many concepts, to learn a reasonable number of highly stable, neatly ordered concepts. In science, however, we need a wide range of materials to teach more concepts, which are less stable and less clearly ordered. These differences between science and other subjects suggest the need for much more support for teachers in this important area of the curriculum.

There is widespread agreement that the aim of science education is conceptual change. Unfortunately, the benchmarks and standards laid out at the national and state levels contain too many concepts for teachers to address in a meaningful way, because conceptual change teaching is time-consuming. According to William H. Schmidt (1997), the national research coordinator for the Third International Mathematics and Science Study, the American curriculum packs in many more topics each year than countries that outperform the United States. He recommends that we pare down the benchmarks and standards.

These limitations restrict the development of science in the elementary curriculum. Elementary teachers, however, do not have to wait for policymakers and curriculum planners to cut down on the number of recommended topics to learn how to do inquiry science. Fortunately, there is less pressure at the elementary level for that kind of coverage than there is at the secondary level. Because inquiry science, which aims for conceptual change, is such a challenge to get off the ground in the elementary schoolroom, a framework is needed for teachers to generate the surprises and insights that lead to further work.

Seven Steps for Organizing Wonder

This chapter sets out the model we have developed for planning and carrying out inquiry science. What follows is, of necessity, a wordy explanation. In actuality, teachers with support and practice can internalize and apply the process in a wide variety of situations. An underlying premise of this framework is that teachers lead and at the same time learn with children rather than follow an outside expert's step-by-step prescription. Once learned, these steps provide a framework comparable to the blueprint teachers carry in their head of the drafting process in writing. Teachers can learn to do "instant science" on the spot.

In order to guide inquiry, a teacher needs experience with the conventions of scientific investigation. We did the first five steps described here as a study group. We worked with the materials ourselves as a group firsthand, while we also introduced them to children. I worked with each teacher individually to go through all of the steps. Sometimes assisting and sometimes team teaching, I helped teachers plan and carry out activities and collect data. In this way we were able to create a forum for planning and reflection. The steps of the approach we recommend follow a general sequence of exploration and investigation. Exploration provides several opportunities to engage in a topic—out of which come questions and ideas for further work. Investigation provides children with an opportunity to examine an idea in detail and systematically. In brief, the steps for organizing wonder are:

Step One: Identify key ideas and experiences on a topic.

Step Two: Search for activities with potential for investigation.

Step Three: Reshape sourcebook activities into explorations.

Step Four: Introduce a series of explorations.

Step Five: Transform children's ideas and questions into questions for investigation.

Step Six: Analyze problem for fair-testing potential.

Step Seven: Ask children to plan, carry out, and interpret investigation.

Step One: Identify Key Ideas and Experiences on a Topic

One of the questions that arises when doing inquiry science is, What topics lend themselves most readily to investigation? First, the materials, objects, events, and living things of everyday life, common to children and teachers, are the stuff of science at the elementary level because children have a wealth of experiences and ideas from which to draw in these areas.

Second, since the goal of investigation is the testing of hypotheses, it is important to chose topics on the basis of their testability. Topics should provide opportunities for:

- observing similarities and differences
- noticing a sequence of events
- identifying patterns and relationships

For example, in the situations at the chapter's beginning, when children shine flashlights through translucent, transparent, and opaque materials, they can observe similarities and differences. After watching a mirror held faceup to the ceiling as they walk through a doorway, they can re-create the sequence of events. They can identify the relation between changing angles of a flashlight and the shape of the resulting pool of light.

The criteria of comparison, sequence, and pattern possibilities indicate potential for the necessary components of investigation:

- fair testing, in which the variable to be changed is the only one that will affect the result (e.g., three kinds of material through which to shine the light, with the one changing variable being the kind of material)

- controlling variables, in which all but one variable is kept the same (e.g., the same flashlight held in the same position)

- measuring or comparing the effect on one variable (e.g., the amount of light that gets through)

In particular, fair testing is necessary to an understanding of science and provides opportunities for open-mindedness and flexible thinking. It is discussed in greater depth further in this chapter.

Third, the main topics of science, like light, provide the most clear-cut opportunities for inquiry, because the knowledge base is well established and easily accessed, and there are many fair-testing opportunities and activities for children described in the literature.

Finally, firsthand manipulation of certain materials can reveal basic scientific ideas that are accessible to children, making an investigation of light traveling in straight lines feasible in fourth grade, while ruling out an investigation of physiological effects of radiation from the electromagnetic spectrum.

For reasons, therefore, of relation to children's experience, fair-testing potential, clear-cut science connections, and accessibility to children's thinking, the topics recommended for starting in inquiry science are light, sound, and forces in the field of physics; the uses and types of materials in the field of chemistry; and the processes of life from biology. These topics are specific to science, yet broad enough that they relate easily to any one of a number of units commonly taught in the elementary school, thus integrating easily into the curriculum. Fortunately for teachers, the science education community has issued recently several developmental guidelines (e.g., the American Association for the Advancement of Science's *Benchmarks for Scientific Literacy* (1993), the National Research Council's *National Science Education Standards* (1996), and state guidelines (e.g., the Massachusetts Core Curriculum and the New Jersey Core Curriculum Standards). After choosing a topic, a teacher can turn to one or more of these guidelines for an orientation.

At the outset of our work together our primary reference was the final draft of the English national science curriculum, *Science for Ages 5 to 16* (Department of Education and Science 1988), the first of these guidelines to appear, and its successors, *Science in the National Curriculum* (DES 1989) and *Science for Ages 5 to 16* (DES 1991). The American guidelines, which are practically interchangeable with each other and with their British counterparts, did not appear until well into the nineties. The draft of the English national curriculum shows practical schoolroom activities and scientific ideas side by side in developmental terms. The draft is the only one of the guidelines, American or British, to align the ideas of science and practice so directly, a presentation we found particularly useful in the beginning when we were struggling to understand what to do with children. Here are the recommended schoolroom activities from the 1988 version (demonstrating *forces*):

> Ages 5–7: In the context of classroom and outdoor play activities children should experience natural and man-made forces which push, pull, make things move, stop things and change the shape of objects. Such experiences could include, for example, road safety activities.

> Ages 7–11: Children should use measurements to compare the effects of forces in the context of, for example, bridge building and investigation of the strength of shapes and structures. They should experience the forces involved in everyday contexts such as transport (including cycling and sailing), balancing systems, and hydraulic mechanisms in model making. (DES 1988)

The ideas or concepts that elementary children are expected to develop are summed up as follows:

> At 5–7 the pupils should know that pushes and pulls can make things move, stop and change.

> At 7–11 pupils should understand that when things are changed in shape, begin to or stop moving, then forces are acting on them. At 7–11 pupils should understand that the movement of an object depends on the magnitude of the force exerted on it, for example in the context of investigations with elastic and wind-powered models. They should understand that the greater the speed of an object the greater the force that is needed to stop it and understand the significance of this for road safety. They should understand that the effect of a force depends on where it is applied in relation to a pivot. They should understand that things fall because of a force of attraction with the Earth (gravity). (DES 1988)

Using these guidelines in their planning as part of Step One, teachers can summarize aspects of forces to pursue with their classes:

- Natural and man-made forces push and pull, make things move, stop things, and change the shape of objects.

- The strength of shapes and structures is researchable.

- Forces exist in everyday contexts, e.g. transport balancing systems and hydraulic mechanisms.

- Movement of an object depends on how much force is exerted on it.

- The greater the speed of an object, the greater the force needed to stop it.

- The effect of a force depends on its relation to a pivot.

- Gravity is a force of attraction with the earth.

Because the guidelines describe in simple language experiences and ideas that children may have about forces, they provide an excellent orientation and starting point for identifying and reworking activities from elementary science texts.

In addition to looking at national, state, or local curriculum guidelines for an orientation, it is important to consult a reference for information about content. In the area of physics, the latest edition of Paul G. Hewitt's *Conceptual Physics* (1987) is particularly accessible.

Step Two: Search for Activities with Potential for Investigation

There is a chasm, however, between these abstractions and what happens in the classroom. If only the teaching and learning of science were as easy as saying, "See what you can find out about the strength of these structures"! Steps Two and Three are a bridge over the chasm between abstraction and activity. In Step Two, the teacher searches for activities that bring these key ideas into play.

Activities and materials for investigating a topic are chosen on the basis of their potential for fair testing. Criteria for investigation potential, as discussed previously, are:

- a range of similarities and differences

- a sequence of events

- patterns and relationships

At this point we gather activity books, children's how-to books, elementary science education textbooks, work cards—every kind of source on the topic we can find. It is critical for teachers without a great deal of experience in hands-on science to have access to these resources. Searching through a set of resources results in several activities that meet the criteria for investigation potential (see Figure 3–1).

Figure 3–1
Science Activity Book

Science Activity Book	Activity
Bathtubs, Slides, Roller Coasters Rails (Lampton 1991)	With a rubber band pull a truck up a short ramp and then a long ramp to the same height to compare the amount of force needed to pull the truck.
Get It in Gear (Taylor 1991)	Make a mobile with straws and different cardboard shapes. Find the pivot or balancing point at each level when adding the next level.
	Slide binder clips, rolls of tape, or paper clips down a string slope. Time the slide. Change the angle of the slope; how do size and weight of object affect speed?
Physics for Every Kid (VanCleave 1991)	Make a straw balance with halved index cards as weights; note changes when cards are moved in their slits.
Raceways: Having Fun with Balls and Tracks (Zubrowski 1985)	Race balls on tracks made of boards and molding. Make a simple stick release and place a board for stopping balls at the end. Sound indicates the winner. Variations: Compare wooden and plastic beads, marbles and ball bearings. Vary height of tracks. Lengthen tracks.
Science Experiences with Everyday Things (Munson 1988)	Tug-of-war: Each side tries to pull toward it the weight of the opponent and the rope; each side tries to overcome force created by friction of the feet of the opponent.
	Make a rubber band gizmo to make fair tests of different forces required to pull cardboard boxes with different weights; try on table and slope.
	Compare strength of forces when things fall: drop marbles from different heights into mud; drop different-sized marbles from the same height.
	Use a spring balance to pull heavy blocks of wood along different surfaces. Is there more friction with some materials than with others?

Step Three: Reshape Source Book Activities into Explorations

Why not simply do these activities as suggested? Unfortunately, the activities are highly directed by the author's hypotheses and questions. Children need several exposures to materials in order to generate their own questions and hypotheses, which can lead, with the teacher's guidance, to fair testing. Each situation needs reworking for that to happen. Motivation, commitment, pleasure, and interest take a quantum leap when children have enough time to generate their own ideas.

In Step Three the teacher changes these activities by creating open-ended exploration questions. Using what-happens-when-you and can-you questions as templates, the sourcebook activities are reworked:

- See what happens when you pull trucks with rubber bands.
- See if you can balance these boards with materials from the junk box.
- What happens when you slide things down a string slope?
- See what happens when you roll balls on these tracks.
- Can you break a paper clip?
- Try sliding loaded checkbook boxes down the ramps.
- Try rolling a marble on different kinds of carpet.
- Try a tug-of-war in pairs.
- Try pulling plastic snow sleds with weights in them.
- What happens when you drop marbles into mud?
- See what happens when you pull loaded, plastic snow sleds on different surfaces.

Each one of these situations has potential in the long run for an investigation in which a variable is changed or an idea is verified through controlled observation.

Step Four: Introduce a Series of Explorations

The work of developing a topic and several explorations is over. Now is the time to introduce the start-up questions to the children. In this phase the teacher needs to constantly note children's observations, hypotheses, and questions. Observations are what children notice when using the senses: similarities and differences, sequence of events, and details relevant to the environment. Hypotheses are simply children's ideas about what is happening. Children sometimes state them in discussion or while working with materials, as when they exclaim, "The heavy balls go fastest." Teachers can push them further in their thinking by asking, "Why do you think some go faster than others?" While some questions may require reference books, and are acceptable, our approach is more concerned with questions that lead to action, such as, "What happens when you roll marbles on different surfaces?" Teachers can note children's observations, hypotheses, and questions on a clipboard as they circulate, on easel paper during a whole-group discussion, or on a tape recorder—making sure to note children's names as a form of assessment. Teachers might also ask an aid, observer, or volunteer to take notes. In this approach assessment drives inquiry: it is built in at every step of the process. Observations, hypotheses, and questions in all phases reveal change in conceptual understanding over the course of the unit of study. That is why this book does not have a separate chapter on evaluation. Assessment is constant feedback that leads to the next step of learning and teaching.

Select a first exploration. At this point, select one of the explorations listed previously.

Set the stage for exploration. With the whole class, set the stage for the exploration by introducing the topic and soliciting children's prior experiences and ideas in a way that engages their interest. Record their experiences and ideas using their language and noting each child's name. Ask, "What do you know about making things move?"

Direct exploration. Next, pose an invitation to exploration. Direct children into small groups or pairs. Discuss safety issues. Explorations are best timed initially to last ten minutes. Short periods of hands-on work followed by discussion enable the teacher to gauge and direct the flow of attention.

Allow children to explore materials openly, even if the children appear to digress. If you are new to hands-on science, consider starting with a small group. Look neutral and interested, and try not to ask many questions or make comments while the children are working. If you need to encourage children, stick first to the very open-ended questions that triggered their work. As you circulate, try to make recordings of children's observations, actions, ideas, and questions. Monitor safety and the proper use of equipment and materials. Look calm.

Keep in mind that some children need to watch and think for a while before taking the plunge to work with materials. Teachers often want to see everybody immediately doing something, but not all students work this way. Also, children often think aloud when working with others. It is common to see them simultaneously thinking aloud while handling materials in a small group or by themselves. Or, they think to themselves while working independently, and do not appreciate having to stop their flow of thought to describe it to the teacher. In some cases, the teacher may think that little productive exploration is going on. However, the discussion following explorations more often reveals that children who looked aloof or side-tracked actually observed relevant details.

Discuss observations, ideas, and questions. Gather the children together for a discussion of their observations. Ask them what they noticed ("What did you notice about ___?") and record their responses in *their* language. Receive all observations without correction and without leading children to observations that you think are most interesting. Language will be simple at the beginning. Children may have difficulty finding words to express their first observations. This is a good time to probe individual students, asking them to find another way of saying what they noticed. After receiving several observations, occasionally solicit children's ideas or hypotheses about observations that appear to you as most relevant to fair-testing situations. This is why it is so important to have prepared carefully in the first three steps. In other words, start focusing on ideas that lead to fair testing, using the more scientific terms generated by individuals in the group. You can do this with a question that takes this form: "Why do you think that ___?" Ask about whatever children had noticed (e.g., that heavy cars go faster than light cars). Try to use the language that the children use, especially when they use the scientific terminology in the state and national curriculum guidelines. Children will use such terms as *push, pull, start-and-stop motion, gravity,* and so on.

Do another round of exploration. Another exploration of the same question after discussion is optional. If your initial exploration was ten minutes, and you had a ten-minute discussion, you may want to explore more before asking students to record observations. In discussion, students generate new ideas they want to try out. They may need to try these out before making recordings.

Ask children to make recordings. From time to time ask children to write down their observations and make diagrams of what they noticed. For example, ask them to show what happens when different balls are dropped in loose sand or when they pull trucks with rubber bands. Ask them to use such devices as labels and arrows to indicate what is happening. You might even ask them to list questions they have about the topic. These notes and diagrams just begin to scratch the surface of all that children observed and thought in explorations. Therefore, especially in the early grades (when writing is so time-consuming), avoid allocating too much importance to recordings. Children should not have to labor too much with these notations. Recordings are like first drafts in writing: best thought of as "sloppy copies."

Do more explorations. Each exploration leads to new exploration. As adults, teachers are strongly tempted to skip further rounds of exploration, because we are often ready to move to fair testing before the children are ready. But children need several exposures to develop ideas about a topic. Also, several explorations build a sense of community and a common focus. Children need to do two or three explorations to become highly focused.

Instead of following explorations that they had identified as part of their planning, teachers can also take one of the children's observations, hypotheses, or questions from their own notes or from the discussion as the basis of the next exploration. Teachers might start the next exploration by saying, "Yesterday ___ noticed that ___. See what you can find out about ___." Here are some anticipated elaborations of the exploration mentioned previously:

- Try pulling the trucks up a long ramp and a short ramp. What is the difference between pulling a truck up a long ramp and a short ramp?

- What happens when you slide binder clips, rolls of tape, and paper clips down a string slope? What difference do you notice?

- What happens when you race different-sized marbles on the tracks? Try plastic and wooden beads. In what ways are they different? In what ways are they alike?

- See if you can break paper clips of different sizes. Which one is strongest?

It is best to follow the lead of children's interests if you can see a fair-testing possibility in the long run. Fortunately, fair-testing opportunities abound any time a set of materials such as these are brought into play.

Through two or three encounters with selected materials, the children will generate ideas and raise questions. The teacher's task is to encourage the children to voice them. As a coach, the teacher draws from a personal understanding of the topic to recognize when more scientific terminology is being used and to model that terminology. Teachers should also recognize when to introduce it if the children do not. Taking time for discussion and journal reflection is critical to the development of more sophisticated thinking about the natural world. In most schoolrooms there are a few children who take to science like candy; their incisive observations and enthusiasm provide excellent models for other children. The more observations and hypotheses that are generated, the better their understanding will be of the variables in the situation. This is the beginning of sustained science activity, which is so rare in our schools.

Step Five: Transform Children's Ideas, Hypotheses, and Questions into Questions for Investigation

Around first and second grade children can begin to move beyond exploration to investigation. Investigation is a systematic study of a problem. Because fair testing involves keeping track of more than one variable, these first attempts are very rough. Remember, elementary children of all ages need extensive opportunities to explore before investigation—much more time than inexperienced adults might think is necessary.

After a few explorations, assemble children's observations, ideas, and questions. Now is the time to identify and transform them into one of these forms:

- Which ___ is best for ___?
- Is it true that ___?
- Which ___ is/does ___? (Harlen and Jelly 1990)

As you move to investigation, it is always best to pay careful attention to what seems to interest children the most. Teachers can take up that interest, which shows up in observations and hypotheses, and forge it into investigation questions, using Harlen and Jelly's forms as templates. The following investigation questions can be anticipated in relation to forces:

- What kind of shoe tread is best for a tug-of-war on the gym floor?
- Is it true that heavy weights close to the pivot balance light weights far from the pivot? Is it true that the force of gravity is greater on large marbles than on small marbles?
- Which ramp, long or short, requires the most force for pulling trucks to the top? Which objects slide the fastest down string

slopes? Which balls go fastest down raceways? Which kind of paper clips are hardest to break?

Because the children have explored the topic more than once, they will have strong ideas about the questions based on their experience. Now is the time to put their hypotheses to a test. This is the critical point in the inquiry for moving forward to fair testing. It is important to know that children can make a plan for testing their hypotheses without a conscious awareness of controlling variables and identifying independent and dependent variables, in much the same way that they can speak without a sophisticated knowledge of grammar. The teacher, however, needs to analyze the situation before proceeding in order to guide the children in a productive direction. Most highly educated adults in our society lack an understanding of fair testing. This is a challenging part of the process of inquiry science, but, like many other skills, once a teacher understands how it works, it is easy.

Step Six: Analyze Problem for Fair-Testing Potential

The next step, then, is for teachers to analyze the investigation questions(s) they plan to introduce for fair-testing potential. An analysis of one of the investigation situations described earlier demonstrates components of fair testing. In the question "What kind of shoe tread is best for a tug-of-war?" the *independent variables* are three different rubber soles with contrasting treads. The *variables to be kept the same or controlled* are the kind of floor and matching students for strength. The *dependent variable* to be measured or compared is the grip ability of the tread. For further discussion of controlling variables, consult Harlen's "Helping Children to Plan Investigations" in *Primary Science* (1985a). Harlen treats investigation as a full-blown possibility at a high level right from the beginning. In contrast to Harlen's beliefs, our approach allows for investigations that are comparable to "sloppy copies" in children's writing.

After children have done investigations, the teacher can call their attention to elements of fair testing. In the early years of elementary school, the question "Was it a fair test?" is enough. In later elementary years, as children gain experience with investigation, the following questions become feasible: "What changed in your test?" "What stayed the same?" "What was measured or compared?" Toward the end of elementary school, when children are highly experienced in investigation, we can introduce the technical language of scientific inquiry—of controlling variables.

Step Seven: Ask Children to Plan, Carry Out,
and Interpret an Investigation

Children work most effectively in planning investigations when they work collaboratively. Group planning puts them in the position of having to reason verbally about a problem. The varying perspectives, understandings, skills, and abilities of group members come into play in this step. The more experience children have with the problem at the exploration stage, the easier it will be for them to plan an investigation. We have found that students are the most highly focused in this phase of the work.

Select an investigation question. There are several ways of proceeding here. The teacher can select one investigation problem for all small groups, small groups can select a problem from several shaped by the teacher or by the whole class, or the whole class can seek consensus on one problem for all small groups to pursue.

Write a plan for the investigation. Ask small groups to make a plan in writing for an investigation. If students say they already know the answer to the question, explain that this is the time to submit an idea to a test. More often than not children continue to discover new aspects of the problem at this higher level of work.

Attach conditions to the plan by asking students to state some or all of the following:

- the question
- the step-by-step plan for the investigation
- a hypothesis
- predictions
- a statement describing measurements to be made and the method for recording measurements
- the independent variable, controlling variable, and dependent variable

The group may stipulate the division of roles.

In the earlier grades it is advisable to start with the statement of the question and a brief step-by-step plan. Then, children may specify predictions and a measurement statement. Toward the end of elementary school, children with prior experience in investigation can begin to use the technical language of fair testing, stating what will stay the same and what will change.

Present plans to the whole class (optional). For many young children (K–2), thought and action go together, making this step an exercise in frustration. Further along, brief presentations can help children to rethink a plan.

Carry out investigations. In this phase, students are highly focused. Troubleshoot by coaching a group through an unexpected glitch in their plan and helping students find materials. Remind students to record their findings.

Summarize findings and present to the class. Ask groups to present their findings to the whole class, perhaps in the form of a chart. Ask students for feedback. Discuss whether or not the investigation was a fair test. From the middle of elementary school, introduce a consideration of fair-testing elements: Was one thing changed? What was it? What was kept the same? Was one thing measured or compared? What was it? Ask students to reflect on what they might have done differently or what they will do in the next investigation that they didn't do in this one.

Make "What do you know about ___?" diagrams. Ask individual students to show what they know about the topic in a diagram. They can use the terminology in the form of labels and arrows and other markers to show what happens. They can communicate what they learned in writing or dictation. Compare the diagrams with their early statements from the beginning of the unit to evaluate conceptual change.

Conclusion

To guide children in inquiry, teachers need to do inquiry firsthand. We explored materials together on several different occasions and learned how to develop questions and hypotheses for further work. We looked at learning goals in the form of developmental standards and provided opportunities for children to change their thinking in the direction of more sophisticated ideas. I worked with each teacher to plan and carry out explorations and investigations. We think this is an important way to start. We learned to use reason and metaphor in relation to the materials at hand; to listen to others' ideas; to consider curriculum guidelines; to reshape our ideas; and to recognize a hypothesis, test it, and draw conclusions.

We found that children often have many more ideas than we have about materials. We learned to learn with each other and to learn with our children about the natural world. Learning collaboratively with peers and children about the natural world feels like a tremendous risk in the beginning, because teachers naturally want to control the learning outcome. While there is a great deal of control in the ways of beginning to work scientifically, as outlined in the framework of the seven steps, the interplay of variables is complex. Investigations seem to raise more questions and often do not work out as hoped. This is to be expected. The process becomes the seedbed for future learning. At the same time, we have evidence that our children's understanding of the natural world becomes more sophisticated. We have come to realize that raising questions, handling variables, and orchestrating a series of explorations that lead to investigation are part of the fun of science.

Chapter Four

Teachers Talking to Teachers
Issues in Getting Started

Occasionally I do hands-on science but not often. I am uncertain about how to direct children's activity. It is clear that they love it. What concerns me, though, are things like spills on the floor, water dumped into larger containers splashing in all directions, water droppers dribbling water. . . . It is all too easy for children to become overexcited when materials are introduced. They often throw their whole bodies into it and excitedly talk to each other and to themselves. I value occasional free exploration but I want children to learn something, and I need to feel in control of what is happening. (Second grade teacher.)

This teacher wants to try inquiry science. She agrees with the aims of our approach—that children should be encouraged to

- generate their own ideas and questions about the natural world
- discuss their work among themselves and in a group as directed by the teacher
- work through several explorations to investigation
- develop more sophisticated ideas about the natural world

She has used variations of these aims in her writing program. Yet she feels overwhelmed in the face of the children's excitement and activity when handling material for science. In this chapter Carol Callahan (grade 3), Helen Kitchel (grade 2), Pat Pierce (grades 4 and 5), Pedie O'Brien (grade 4), and Jody Hall address the issues raised by this teacher in a dialogue format. Included in the discussion is Lisa Beck, a first-grade teacher who worked with us.

The Issue of Control

Teachers need to feel confident that learning is going on in a classroom. In the inevitable flurry of children's high-speed interactions with the "stuff" of the world and the constant stream of excited talk, a teacher may doubt that learning is taking place. We have found, however, that after orienting students with an initial exploration question, teachers need to let go and to trust children, without ignoring issues of safety and the proper use of materials. We have found that the first exploration can seem the most chaotic. We struggled with the issue of control, especially at the beginning of our work together.

Pedie O'Brien: Until children get used to handling materials in a group situation, there is a little bit of confusion, at least it seems there is. It takes time for teachers to learn how to direct this kind of learning. It is not something you can do instantaneously. I had to give up the feeling of needing complete control over what the children thought and did. Before I taught this way, I had to tell them exactly what they were going to learn in the situation. But, I noticed that what they found out and what I expected them to find out did not match. They have their own ideas.

Helen Kitchel: Children who are exploring something for the first time, especially exciting materials instead of a book to read, get really wound up. For example, I set up an initial exploration of waves for my second graders. They had rubber tubes, a long metal coil, and three water tables for materials. We started with a brainstorming session on what they knew about waves. And then I said, "See what happens when you make waves with these materials." What followed next felt like chaos to me. In retrospect perhaps I should have done it on the playground, because the big wave action of long rubber tubes and coils and the messiness of making water waves seemed so out of control. The wave motion of big tubes and big coils, with one person at one end and one at the other, creates a high degree of energy.

During the exploration I felt very anxious, because there were children in the hall with tubes and coils. There was water on the floor, and I was worried someone would trip and fall. Learning to make waves was more of a challenge than I had anticipated. Later, however, after a couple of explorations, children were able to work at the water table in a very controlled manner. They had learned how to make waves that they could observe, and at the same time keep the water in the water table.

Carol Callahan: There are a lot of ways you can control the activity. When my children explored forces while doing a tug-of-war in pairs, there was extraordinary action. I saw children pulling with all their might. They got their whole bodies into it. Some were crashing to the floor. I even saw some gesturing with ropes around their necks! I decided then and there to limit their exploration to a few short sessions interspersed with discussion. After a few minutes, I said, "OK, we're stopping now. We're going to report on it. Put the ropes down and sit down." After a short discussion, which included brief attention to safety issues, they would go at it again, followed by a few minutes of discussion. The teacher can control the activity.

Lisa Beck: Recently my first graders were exploring forces with marbles. They were rolling them on different surfaces and down inclines. Watching them, I wondered what other people must think when they go by the door and look in. Do they think it is chaos? Do they think that children are not learning? People who don't understand this approach might wonder. In the beginning I wondered myself about this kind of free exploration. But, gathering the children back on the rug at the end of that kind of learning experience, I always found out that they had learned a great deal. I asked, "What did you notice? What happened? What did you just discover?" If the teacher doesn't use these kinds of questions to start a discussion, she won't realize how much children are learning.

Helen Kitchel: We did a guided discovery on balls before our exploration; we discussed how to use the balls in a safe, caring, and learning way. Children stated their ideas on how this could be accomplished as I listed them on chart paper. Then they practiced them by role playing. At the end of each role play, children made specific comments on what they saw each other doing. This created a productive atmosphere for exploring exciting materials.

The Question of Whether or Not to Limit Early Exploration

One of the questions that often arises is how much to limit exploration to the question posed at the beginning of the hands-on work. This issue is of particular concern in the first exploration of a unit of study, before students have built up much understanding of the materials at hand. The teacher decides what materials to set out and what aspects of the topic to emphasize in the opening activity, but when children engage with the materials, their questions drive the work. The following comments show a range of views on this issue.

Carol Callahan: I had a situation in which students were supposed to be observing the properties of paper. Among other things, I put containers of water on the tables. Well, of course many of them immediately went to the water and were dunking bits of construction paper into the water. They started making different colors in the water.

Lisa Beck: I've learned a good technique for focusing my first graders. We begin with a discussion about different ways they can go about exploring a topic. They have some choices, but one choice they do not have is going off and choosing a different subject or a different topic. For example, if the question is "How can we find which of these papers is the strongest paper?" then exploring the color properties of paper is not a way of working on that question. Restating the question is a quick redirect. When we were doing properties of fabric, the children were observing the magnification property of water instead of looking at properties of fabric. I directed their attention to what they noticed about the magnified fabric.

Pedie O'Brien: But you can't just discourage that. You might say, "That is interesting. Go ahead and see what you can find out about that." Alternatively, you might redirect the child and plan for exploration in this area at another time.

Carol Callahan: I take a different approach at the beginning of exploration. When I put things out, I pretty much let them go. I let them do what they want. If I don't want them to use water, I don't put it out. If I do put it out, they can use it any way they want. It is free exploration. However, when we have the discussion, I ask them to tell me something about the properties of paper. Sometimes what may appear irrelevant at the time to me may be relevant. Some paper actually falls apart in water, like toilet paper, and some dyes used to color the paper are water soluble. I do give them the opportunity to explore freely, but then I start to be more directive. In the discussion I listen to all observations, but generally I try to ask only questions that are the focus of the activity.

Lisa Beck: One of the things I have been experimenting with this year is what to put out and how much to put out. When we were discovering how things move, I just gave them a start-up question and a marble. I did not put out ramps at that point. I did not put out cars or paper tubes. I limited the materials to a question and a marble. And I got wonderful results. The children had their imaginations and their ideas, and they applied them to that one marble!

Pat Pierce: On the other hand, you can start with a huge range of learning opportunities. For example, I start my pond unit with a collecting trip to the pond. The whole pond is there. The students bring back samples of water and samples of plants and animals. Then, in the classroom, they narrow the focus from the whole pond to the samples. So it is a wide study narrowing down to a more limited study. I think we can be open at the pond, explore the whole thing, and then narrow the study in the classroom.

Discussion: A Forum for Learning

We all pause frequently for discussion. We believe that children are able to observe many more details and generate many more ideas than they can record in writing, diagraming, charting, or graphing. Therefore the teacher pauses regularly to discuss work-in-progress with individuals, with small groups, or with the whole class. We place minimal emphasis on recording, especially at the outset of sustained work on a topic.

Jody Hall: That little "What did you notice?" question that we use to start the discussion after hands-on work is a radical question.

Lisa Beck: It turns minds on, it really does.

Pedie O'Brien: Learning has a different meaning with this kind of science. When we ask them questions like these, they have to think for themselves. They have to get in touch with themselves. At first they don't seem to realize that their thoughts are being considered as important. They expect that the only thing the teacher wants is the right answer. Otherwise be quiet.

Carol Callahan: Before I did science this way, I thought that learning occurred when I asked my third graders to reflect on their work in their journals. What I have come to realize is that they can't possibly write out all the ideas that occur to them as they explore and investigate. They are much better in the follow-up discussion. A comment made by one student sets another student off with another idea. Of course, they do make some recordings, but I have come to value the exchange of ideas that occurs in the discussion as a critical factor in science work.

Pat Pierce: I used to wonder whether or not my fourth and fifth graders were learning anything during an exploration. If you don't have a discussion, you won't find out what they learned. I often begin the next session with the discussion of the previous exploration by asking, "What do you know about ___?" Even if a couple of weeks have gone by, the students remember a lot of specific details.

Pedie O'Brien: I would say, "Remember when we did this? What do you remember?"

Lisa Beck: I would add, "Do you have any new ideas about this topic?"

Pedie O'Brien: Or, if a student had been absent the day we did the exploration, I might say, "Who can tell (the student who was absent) what we did?" You get a lot from that, because the audience is fresh.

Carol Callahan: Often I will begin a discussion by describing in specific terms what children said or did in the previous session. For example, "I remember I saw Joey flicking a marble. I think he was doing that for about twenty minutes. Wow! What were you noticing, Joey?" Also, they enjoy hearing me remember specific things they said and did. Sometimes I direct their attention to certain aspects of the topic by focusing on relevant observations that I can see will lead to investigation.

Lisa Beck: The discussion opens up the door. It triggers their memories. The next day after my first graders worked with the marbles, I started a discussion about what they noticed. Laura ran to her backpack and got different objects she had tried at home. What she showed us sparked a discussion connecting her example and the work we had done on the previous day.

Learning to Be a Good Listener

Good discussion occurs only when the teacher is listening very carefully. After a teacher raises a question like "What did you notice?" she is going to hear some ideas.

Jody Hall: In the beginning I remember how hard it was to be open and listen. I would bite down on my tongue and try to look interested. While the student was speaking, I would be having a little inner dialogue between my old teacher "hat" and my new one along the lines of "Keep your mouth shut. I am listening to this student. I want to understand where this student is coming from. Stop having so many of your own ideas about every word that comes out of this student's mouth. You don't have to be telling, directing, and asking questions all the time."

I have become genuinely fascinated with the ideas the students have. I think there is much more real dialogue now in my relations with students. Listening makes teaching more interesting. Also, I learned that children, when doing hands-on work, need time to pursue their own questions without my always being in their face asking questions. Or if they are in a discussion, they need time to think out loud without being cut off. I knew previously about the importance of "wait time," but now I have a better understanding of the direction of discussion. I can lead more focused discussions as a result.

Pedie O'Brien: The way I used to teach, I thought I had to know everything that was going on. I thought I had to be talking and telling all the time, rather than listening.

Carol Callahan: I was great at listening—that was never my problem. I could just listen and listen. But, I was listening for them to come up with the right answer, so then we could move on. Here I was listening; we would be looking at each other. Then I would think, "Now where do I go?" When we started doing science this way, I realized that I wasn't listening well enough so that I could put together their ideas. I wasn't listening well enough so that I could recognize how to respond—with a comment or a question. So, active listening is what I have learned.

As a way of understanding and keeping a record of the children's ideas, we often repeat what each says and write it down on a piece of easel paper or on the chalkboard. Writing down the children's ideas is another way of forcing the teacher to listen to and understand a child's thought.

Pedie O'Brien: I sometimes rephrase. I do it because I think some children have a hard time expressing themselves. Also I want to make sure that I am understanding what they are saying, and I want the rest of the class to understand. In turn the children can say, "Well, no. That is not what I meant."

Carol Callahan: I think it should be repeating but not rephrasing. Repeating what they said is a way of making sure we are not putting it into our own words and thoughts. In fact, repeating is a way of asking, "Is that what I heard you say?" A lot of times repeating helps them to say, "No, that is not what I said." This kind of exchange gives both students and teachers time and space to think the ideas over. In this way we can build a new sense of where we are going.

Pat Pierce: You are clarifying it for yourself.

Children Talking and Learning

We have found that children need to talk to themselves and to each other while they work. They need to do this to think, but it adds to the impression that hands-on work is chaos. A room of twenty or more students handling materials and talking is a dynamic place.

Pedie O'Brien: When I did this at the beginning of our work, it was one of the first times as a teacher that I really let my kids think out loud. At first having them think out loud seems like chaos. I thought, "My goodness, they are thinking out loud! They shouldn't be doing that. They are all talking! They are not doing a thing!" I have come to realize that they are learning, but as a teacher it takes experience to get used to it.

Sustaining Science Activity and Moving to the Investigation Phase

Once a teacher gets accustomed to orchestrating explorations on a topic, science activity can be sustained so that children's ideas and questions can drive inquiry, with coaching from the teacher, in the direction of investigation.

Carol Callahan: Each unit is a learning experience for me. I was not a science major. I read my little books to get a ballpark idea of the topic. I develop a general idea of the variables, but as I plunge in a lot more appear. Together the students and I move beyond our original sense of the topic. It is very exciting to learn so much with students.

Jody Hall: I am particularly struck by the growth of language when science activity is sustained. At first the language is not very descriptive; often the sentences are fragmentary and accompanied by body gestures. In discussions we repeatedly ask them to describe what they observe in more detail. Language becomes more elaborate.

Carol Callahan: The talking among children is important, too. If they're going to make a wave that is three segments, for example, they have to talk it over. They have to come to an agreement about what they are looking for and how to do it.

Pedie O'Brien: At the beginning, especially, I spent a lot of time getting that perfect question that was going to lead to action or to children's saying what is on their minds. [For this we made repeated reference in particular to the Jelly and Elstgeest chapters in Harlen's *Primary Science: Taking the Plunge*.]

Carol Callahan: In the beginning I was scared because I was not accustomed to thinking with students. I have learned to relax and go with the flow. At first in working like this we put our toes in and said, "It's not too bad so far. Do I dare go up to my ankles? Let's see what happens."

Pedie O'Brien: This approach seems to me a natural way of teaching and learning, rather than contrived, because it is the way we learn. Sometimes as teachers we contrive things to teach a concept. As a learner I need to touch and feel things, and experiment. As I begin to find out more, I get excited and want to do more. Kids are really excited when they can find out things on their own.

Jody Hall: As far as fair testing and controlling variables go—one thing changing and keeping everything else the same—I think we got to the point where we could begin to think in those terms.

Carol Callahan: As soon as children take the initiative in answering their own questions, I believe that they are getting into the investigation phase. They make a little plan, which may or may not get expressed. The more they do it, the more refined awareness of the variables they have.

Helen Kitchel: Right from the start of a unit, I notice varying levels of questions. Some are already asking questions related to a hypothesis that they are trying to prove or disprove, though they may have difficulty putting their thoughts into words. While watching them at work and listening to their talk, I can see that they are at this level. Others are still in the exploration stage—making observations by comparing, sequencing, or finding patterns. But they are not yet trying to answer an investigation kind of question, such as which is the best ball for bouncing. The role of the teacher is to give them opportunities to explore and investigate and to ask them to put their thoughts into words. The teacher may need to frame the investigation question for younger children.

Carol Callahan: Toward the end of units I find we can talk about variables. The more time we spend on it, the more serious we become. We have to watch more carefully. I do my best to follow their ideas and questions. I give them a chance to think it through—to make the connections.

Helen Kitchel: I find that after they have plenty of time with exploration, second graders are able to write a focused plan and carry it out.

Carol Callahan: As a teacher I believe I have to get younger children to talk through their plan. Many little ones in first through third grades don't plan through or visualize what they going to do in a detailed way. I prompt by asking, "Who is going to be your partner? How are you going to stand?" After they do it we talk again, and they decide that the next time they are going to stand closer to each other. Each time it is more refined. They are thinking and learning as they experiment.

I think it is important to emphasize that the written plans use simple language, and that the verbal expression as they work and discuss with each other and in groups is much more sophisticated. It takes them a long time to say very little in writing.

Pedie O'Brien: There is another issue: not having enough time because of needing to meet the schedule. It is often difficult to be as flexible as you want to be.

Carol Callahan: As a teacher I know how to lead children in a process of working through to a deeper understanding. It does take time and unfortunately can't be done as much as I would like because of other demands on my time. I think it is important, though, that I know how to do it.

The teacher quoted at the beginning of the chapter expressed concern about managing inquiry science and making sure that children learn something. We had these concerns ourselves when we started doing science. In the first two years we met frequently to have these kinds of discussions. By working in tandem on explorations and investigations and by bringing examples of children's work to our meetings, we worked through the issues that arise when doing inquiry science that leads to conceptual change.

In the next four chapters, each teacher describes a unit of study in depth. The work reported follows the seven steps outlined in Chapter 3.

Chapter Five

What's in a Wave?

Carol Callahan

At the beach a wave goes in, and then it slows down. Then it gets smaller, and [when] it goes back out it hits another wave coming in, and then it joins up with that wave.

This statement was made by one of my third-grade students. She was connecting our study of waves with her own experience. In the schoolroom, we made our own waves with materials such as loose-coiled springs and different lengths of rope. The following exchange—early in our work on this topic—occurred after the students had made waves with thin, red rubber tubing.

Carol: What kind of wave or waves did you make? How many? What can you tell us? Table One, would you like to show us and, while you show us, explain what you observed?

Student: A tidal wave [she says while making one with her group].

Carol: Wow! A tidal wave. Show us, again. [Students demonstrate.] So what are we seeing here? Who can put some words to this?

Student: The vibration is pretty strong when they make it go up and down.

Student: At first we held the end in our hand.

Carol: You hold it another way now?

Student: I wrapped it around my hand, or it will fly away.

Carol: What happens when you make a wave?

Student: It's going up and back.

Carol: So, it's going up and back. How else could we describe that?

Student: It's like it goes up to the shore and back out?

Student: It makes a big wave, like in the real waves. They come back with short ones and then they come back.

Carol: So "up and back from the shore" and a big wave goes up and it comes back in smaller waves?

Student: [Nods in the affirmative that what I said was right.]

In the early phases of our work on a topic, I have to listen very carefully to what they say, repeat it, and sometimes get them to rephrase. I use their language and encourage them to refine it. I pose open questions to help children use their higher-order thinking skills and explore further. Time and again I have learned that children notice relevant details that I had not anticipated. As we proceed to work together, we begin to zero in on specific ideas, or hypotheses, and questions for investigation. It is a process of working through to understanding. This chapter shows how children's ideas and questions lead to new discoveries.

Background Information for a Study of Waves

For our study of waves I supplied the children with materials that would allow them to explore the different kinds of waves (transverse, longitudinal, and standing); observe the common characteristics of each wave (crest, trough, amplitude, wavelength, and frequency); and create phenomena such as interference patterns and the Doppler effect. I consulted Paul G. Hewitt's *Conceptual Physics* (1987) to get a better understanding of what we were learning in the areas of motion and forces. *Science in the National Curriculum* (Department of Education and Science and the Welsh Office 1989) designates this area of study as "forces" and suggests that students can:

- understand that pushes and pulls can make things start moving, speed up, swerve, or stop
- understand that when things are changed in shape, begin to move, or stop moving, forces are acting on them
- understand that the movement of an object depends on the size and direction of the forces exerted on it
- understand that the greater the speed of an object the greater the force and/or time that is needed to stop it.

Another source, *National Science Education Standards* (National Research Council 1996), calls this area "position and motion of objects" in the field of "Physical Science," and suggests that children can understand the following "fundamental concepts and principles":

- An object's motion can be described by tracing and measuring its position over time.

- The position and motion of objects can be changed by pushing or pulling. The size of the change is related to the strength of the push or pull.

The materials that we worked with included: various lengths of rubber and plastic tubing, loose-coiled springs (about the size of a large jump rope), Slinkys, different lengths of rope, vacuum cleaner hoses, dominoes, ceramic and plastic tiles, and a water table. In addition to consulting curriculum guidelines in the areas of motion and forces, I also consulted them in the area of materials. *Science in National Curriculum* (1989) designates this area "types and uses of materials" and suggests that children can:

- recognise important similarities and differences, including hardness, flexibility, and transparency, in the characteristics of materials

- group materials according to their characteristics

- make comparisons between materials on the basis of simple properties, strength, hardness, flexibility, and solubility

- relate knowledge of these properties to the everyday use of materials

The National Research Council (1996) calls this area "properties of objects and materials" in the field of "Physical Science" and says that the children can learn these ideas:

- Objects have many observable properties, including size, weight, shape, color. . . . Those properties can be measured using tools such as rulers, balances, and thermometers.

- Objects are made of one or more materials, such as paper, wood, and metal. Objects can be described by the properties of the materials from which they are made, and those properties can be used to separate or sort a group of objects or materials.

The classroom is organized to provide a large open space for hands-on work and for class meetings on the rug in front of an easel. Table groups of four sit at tables set up along two walls of the room.

First Thoughts About Waves

I began by asking my second- and third-grade students what they knew about waves. These were some of their thoughts:

> Water. At the beach waves come in. Something to float on—I get swept away by the waves. Bumpy water. Getting washed away. They float me away. When a whale jumps. Ocean and sea. Dolphins—because they ride the bow waves. Dad holds me up so the waves don't get me. The tide. Seashells get washed ashore by waves. I can make waves in my bathtub. People make waves while watching a football game. We wave good-bye. I have wavy hair.

Initial Exploration of Waves

I believe the initial exploration and discussion should be free—no-holds-barred, even if the students have taken off into seemingly tangential directions. For example, in the first discussion after hands-on work, a student noted that a bungee cord is like the long Slinky. One student associated the coil with the wire in her mouth, which connected braces in the lower jaw with braces in the upper jaw. We spent a couple of minutes considering the function of the wire before returning our attention to our discussion of waves. I might have closed off any consideration of the wire, but I feel this initial experience hooks students to the whole scientific process because it allows them to generate their own ideas. I see this as the beginning of their empowerment as learners.

After hearing their first thoughts about waves, we formed a circle on the rug. Pairs of students were asked to make waves with one of the materials, while the rest of us watched. I wanted to control the first work and create a sense of importance for the act of observation. I started this first exploration by picking up on a point made in the "first thoughts" session. I said, "So you think something creates a wave. You think a wave doesn't create itself all by itself? There's something else doing something to the water that creates it?" To which a student responded, "It starts in the ocean and it goes up the beach; then it's really fast." I asked that student to pick a partner and make a wave in the middle of the circle. Three pairs in turn made waves, and I assured the others that they would have their chance soon to make their own waves. I asked everyone to describe what they were observing. Before table teams made waves, I summed up their observations, using their language: "What we have said about people making waves is that they use different movements with their hands, arms, and shoulders. We have seen up-and-down movement with the arms and wrist, we have seen circular movement with the arms and shoulders, and we have seen back-and-forth movement with the shoulders." Then the table groups proceeded to do explorations on their own for twenty to thirty minutes. This is a long time for an exploration, but their interest was high.

At one point we stopped to discuss safety, because students were stretching and releasing the stretchy rubber tubing and overextending the coils. "In our work we are going to be handling these materials," I always say. "What would be a safe way to handle them?" They make the rules.

During the discussion following hands-on work we began to identify variables—without calling them "variables" per se—that affect the inquiry and raise questions for further work. I put a clean piece of paper on the easel and asked the children to tell me what they had found out about waves. Each team demonstrated their findings. These are some of the things they had to say:

> Waves can go up and down and sideways. They can bounce. Waves don't have to be made out of water. If you shake a Slinky, it looks like the waves are walking on the rug. Waves can look like inchworms. Waves can wrestle—one can hit the other and knock it over. If you blow water in a tube with the end up, the water comes out like a spout. It looks like a wave traveling through the tube. Waves can meet and then bounce back the way they came and back again. Sometimes they form one big wave. Sometimes one goes over the other. The harder the pull down on the spring, the longer the waves will keep going.

As children articulate what they did, they gain a greater awareness of what they have learned. I gain an understanding of what they have learned. We are developing a common language. Once I hear a certain tone of confidence, then I know the time is right to introduce more scientific language. Now they will welcome it.

The discussion revealed a high degree of interest in the influence of one wave upon another. I suggested that perhaps we needed to take a closer look at what happens when two waves meet.

Diagraming Waves

Before proceeding to the exploration of waves that meet, we did diagrams and did an exploration of the materials being used. Young children need to understand the difference between scientific diagrams and creative drawing.

Carol: What I want to do right now is give everybody a piece of paper. Today we are going to do a kind of scientific drawing. I want you to make *diagrams*. How do you think you can show the movement of a wave? How can you show the workings of a wave?

Student: Sometimes I just make lines on a ball.

Carol: Show with little marks that it's moving? Can you show us up here on the easel paper? [Student demonstrates.] Who else? How are you going to show that movement has been taking place?

Student: I would use more than one picture. I'd make some squares on the paper. Like if the wave started here, in the next picture it would be there. [Student demonstrates.]

Carol: So if you show then that #1 is here, #2 is here, and #3 is here? [Student nods yes.] OK, so that's another way of showing movement.

Student: You could make an arrow showing where the wave is going. [Student demonstrates.]

Carol: So you're showing that the wave started here and moves in this direction and then back with arrows going both ways. These diagrams are marvelous! I want each of you to make a diagram right now. And then we'll share some more. You can do any kind of wave we made today. What I want to see is what you have noticed about making waves that you can show in a diagram. We haven't been working with ocean waves in our work. I want to see what you have been doing with waves right here. [See Figures 5–1 through 5–3.]

Later that evening, as I went over my notes, I confirmed that much curiosity and enthusiasm had indeed been generated during the children's exploration. The question of what happens when two waves meet seemed a logical next step given the amount of attention it received. Students gave good verbal accounts of what they observed.

It is important to always be on the look out for hypotheses in the students' statements. I noticed in Meg's statement, "The harder the pull down on the spring, the longer the waves keep going," a beginning hypothesis that could lead to further exploration and eventual investigation. Her hypothesis could be turned into an investigation question: "Is it true that the harder the pull down on the spring, the longer the waves keep going?" I thought, however, that the class still needed more time to explore. In the early stages of science work, some students come up with investigation questions immediately, but most need more time to become familiar with the possibilities.

An Exploration of Materials

Before moving on to an exploration of the meeting of waves, I wanted the students to have an opportunity to relate the properties of the materials to their value as wave makers. I asked them to make

Figure 5–1
Chris

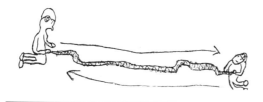

predictions about which of the materials was best for making waves, and I asked them to say why they thought that material was the best. After making predictions, they observed materials in action. The properties that seemed important to various students at that point were no knots, grip ability, length, thinness, hollowness, flexibility, and weight. They concluded that the red rubber tubing and the metal coils were best, because of their grip ability and flexibility.

Exploration of Two Waves Meeting

I asked, "What happens when two waves that are not the same size meet?" The children worked only with the rubber tubing or the metal coils. Here are two of the students' write-ups for the exploration.

Plan

1. We will use the silver coile. 2. Kyra and Alice are going first. 3. Alice will make the bigger wave. 4. Alice will use her whole arm. We thingk that it will cause Alice's wave to be bigger and Kyra's wave to be smaller. [Predictions] 5. Kyra thinks the wave will bounce back and will go back were they started. 6. Krissa thaig the wave will meet and bais back. 7. Alice thingks bothe waves will meet and bounce back. 8. Alec thingks bothe waves will stop and noting will hapin.

Figure 5–2
This is me and Kristen making a wave.

This   is   me   and   Kristen   macking   a   wave.   Marg 5-25.

Figure 5–3
Alex

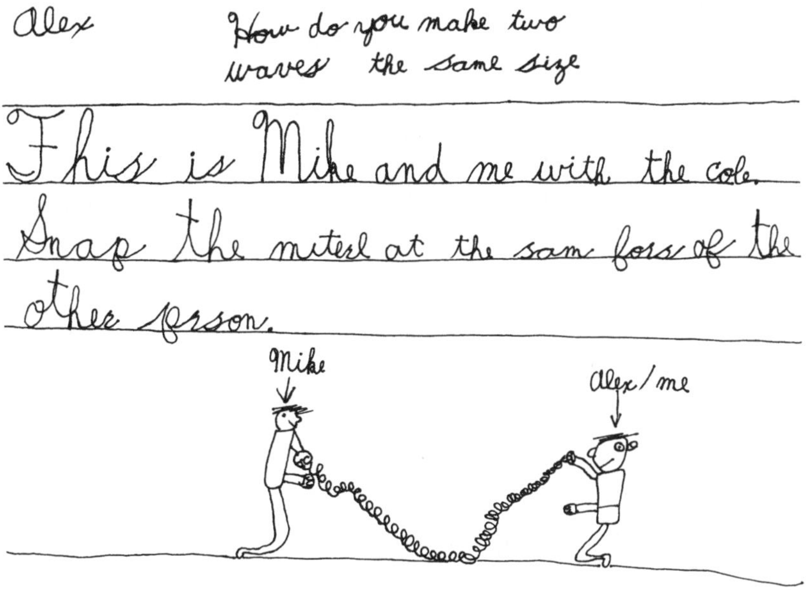

Alex   How do you make two
         waves   the same size

This is Mike and me with the cole.
Snap the mitesl at the sam foss of the
other prson.

Mike

alex/me

Plan

1. We will yous the gold colle. 2. William and Charles are makeing the waves first. 3. Charles is going to mack the big wave. 4. Charles will rase his hand to 39 inch. And William will rase the coil to 25 inchis. [Predictions] 1. I think the big one will go over the small one. 2. they will bace off each other

Individual students wrote up these findings: "The small and big waves met and boused back and turened the same size." "I saw that they bounsed off eouther [each other] or went threw eouther." "I say the big wave and the little wave baws of each other And than when they were going back they sruk [shrunk]."

I asked my students if they had controlled the size of the waves and they all said that they did, using the "same time," "same force," and "same power." I asked, "Are you saying that keeping time and force the same will make the waves the same size?"

"Yes," replied Sandy.

"How do you make waves small?" I questioned. She responded, "You don't use as much power for the little ones."

When I questioned where the power was coming from, she replied, "From your arm. The power comes from your arm."

Jason then said, "There's more! I raise my arm higher when I want a bigger wave but not so high for the smaller wave."

"Yes," said Sandy. "That's how you get the power."

Kyra added, "Also how fast you bring your arm down. I get more force when I bring my arm down fast."

I then asked, "Kyra, what do you mean by the word *force?*"

"Let me show you," she said. What ensued was about thirty minutes of time in which the whole class, myself included, worked together, continuing our discussion about the variables involved in making waves. The class concluded that the size of the wave, and sometimes the number of waves, makes a difference when two waves meet. Students noted:

They met, bounced away, and got smaller.

The bigger one went over the smaller one, then both got a little bigger, but gradually both got smaller.

The bigger one took the smaller one back where the smaller one came from.

Two big ones came to the middle and stopped.

When they are the same size, they stop. When they are a different size, they continue.

> The bigger one ate the smaller one, got even bigger, and went back where it came from.
>
> If you have one big one and five or six small ones, the small ones will push back the big one.

The next morning we resumed our work by reviewing what had been done the previous day. The class discussed their observations that the whole body was involved in making waves, but that the primary action came from the arm and the wrist. We concluded that the speed, height, force, and type of wrist and arm motion determined the size, speed, force, amount, duration, and kind of wave that would be made. I found myself wondering if Newton had made his discoveries about motion when he was eight years old. One of the children then asked if she could "see how many kinds of waves we can make." I said I thought it was a great idea. I also asked them to make diagrams of each wave and write down how they made it. Brad wondered if it was OK to give a name for each wave, and I said I thought that was a good thing to do, too.

How Many Kinds of Waves Can We Make?

Each group selected its materials, made waves, and wrote up the results on a chart. For example, Table Three's chart consisted of four columns. The column headings were *Name, Little Waves, Big Waves*, and *Number of Waves*. In the rows they wrote the name of each wave; checked if it was big or little (sometimes both); and recorded the number of segment waves, if any, they had made. Each group shared only two of the waves that they had made, and only those waves that no other table group had presented.

Individually they wrote descriptions of how one of their waves was made. These were edited for a hallway display. Here are some of their descriptions:

> We counted to three and when we got to three we moved our arms like they were throwing tennis balls sky high and it makes a Tidal Wave.
>
> To make a Foot Wave somebody stands on the coil while holding on to one end of the coil and they pull on the coil away from their foot and the person takes their foot off the coil and it makes a wave.
>
> Mandy and Shel were swinging their arms in a circular motion Then Nerf came and jumped rope three times. We called it the Nerf Wave. (Nerf is one of our school custodians of whom the children are fond.)

We twirled our arms the same direction but different speeds. It made a wave look like glasses. We called it a Glasses Wave.

As each group demonstrated what they had done that morning, the children became progressively more interested in how to "make more than one wave go at once."

Making More than One Wave

"Yesterday we got interested in how to 'make more than one wave go at once,' " I noted. "Before we do an exploration of this, I want us to spend some time this morning talking about what our question would be. How do you make a wave with more than one part? Any other ideas?" The students came up with several versions of the question. At the end we had a list up on the easel:

1. How do you make a wave with more than one part?
2. How do you make more than one wave go at once?
3. How do you make a wave with more than one X?
4. How do you make a wave with more than one loop?
5. How do you make a double, triple, or quadruple wave?
6. How do you make segment waves?

I noted that we had different ways of saying the same idea, and that was fine. With these questions in mind we went to the playground to make multiple waves.

Several variables surfaced in the discussion following the exploration, though we did not use the term *variable* at the time. I have highlighted what I think are the most important aspects of our exchange:

Student: The way you move your arm and wrist makes a difference.

Student: Timing is important. You start out together and one person starts getting a little closer.

Student: You have to get closer together and go really, really fast.

Student: You have to be not too close, not too far, and you have to go very, very fast.

Student: It also matters how heavy they are and how long. It's hard to made doubles and triples with the black rubber one because it's solid in the middle. The red one is good because it's hollow.

Student: Longer is better because when you get closer there's more waves.

Student: It won't go as good if it's heavy. And you can't do it with the red tubing with knots.

Carol: We all have different ideas.

Student: You don't want a really long one and you don't want a really short one.

Carol: What about knots?

Student: Knots don't make any difference.

Student: It adds weight in a certain area.

Student: But it's the same amount of rubber so it's the same weight.

Student: The knots bend it in a different way.

Student: Waves with more than one part have an "x" in the middle.

Student: It's easy to make a double wave but it's harder to make a triple or quadruple wave.

Carol: Why do you think triples and quadruples are harder to make?

Student: Because you need to twirl faster and get closer.

Student: You have to be not too close, not too far. You have to be just perfect and you have to go very, very fast.

Carol: You guys are wonderful! You're coming up with some great ideas: You can't have it too heavy or too light. You can get good control if it's light and flexible. Knots might make a difference. Timing is important, or how fast you move your arm, and the distance between people makes a difference. So, you are all saying that there is more involved in making a wave than just your arm and wrist?

Students: Yes!

This exchange brought into play almost the full range of variables affecting the creation of waves. The distance between people generated the most interest. At this point I decided to move into a formal discussion of variables, noting that we had identified them in our discussion. I wrote "Variables in Making a Wave" on the easel paper. By the end of this session we had a chart with a more precise title of "Variables in Making Waves with Rubber Tubing and Metal Coils," listing the variables of thickness, weight, length, speed, flexibility, and distance.

When I placed *distance* on the chart, we talked about what that might mean. I said, "Randy, show me what you mean by *close*. I'll hold one end of the tubing." He took the other end of the tubing and stood "close" to me. I then walked a few steps closer and asked, "Is this also close?" Everyone shook their heads yes. I said, "So which close do we mean when we say *close*, and how about *medium* and *far*?" Joe laughed and said, "OK, OK, we get the point. We need to measure!" The children decided we should write the words *yards, feet,* and *inches* under the "Distance" heading.

An Investigation

That night I made plans for the children to launch into an investigation. I decided that the question I would pose to them would be, "Using a piece of rubber tubing, what is the best distance to have between people while making a wave with three segments?"

The following day, I placed two easels side by side. I wrote the question to be investigated on one easel and placed the wave variables chart on the other. After reading the question to the children, I then asked them to tell me what material they would be using for the investigation. They quickly came up with "rubber tubing," which I underlined within the investigation question. Then I placed a check mark next to "rubber tubing" on the variables chart. My next question was, "What are you being asked to make?" When they gave me the answer, I underlined "a wave with three segments" and then asked them which one of the variables on the chart we were trying to find out about. One student said, "Distance. We don't know that yet. We need to find out. That's what we have to figure out." He then carefully read the investigation question aloud to the class, giving special emphasis to "what is the best distance to have between people." I then proceeded to help the children set up their investigations:

> So let's see. We know that the material you will be using is rubber tubing. The desired outcome or what you need to make is a three-segment wave, and to make that wave you need to find out the best distance between people. That is the question you will be investigating. So when you are through with your investigation, you will put in some numbers in yards, feet, and inches.
>
> Before you begin your investigation you will need to write a plan. You will write the plan with the other members of your table group. I would like the paper monitor to please give each table one piece of long, yellow, lined paper. Decide on who will do the writing. Once you have chosen a writer and have all of your names and the date on your paper, I will give you more directions.
>
> OK. I can see that everyone is ready to go on. The next thing you will write on your paper is, "Plan for Investigation." Your names are on the top line, so skip a line from there and then write, "Plan for Investigation." Then please skip a line and write, "Material being used—rubber tubing." I will demonstrate on the chalkboard.
>
> Looking at our variables chart, I can see that we have a number of things listed under "Rubber Tubing." Which of these will stay the same?

In the course of the discussion, we agreed that thickness, weight, speed, and length needed to stay the same. The children would use the rubber tubing and keep the speed the same when testing different distances. They then proceeded to plan and carry out their investigations. When the whole class looked at the results, they could see that each group had identified different distances as best for producing three-part waves. It was noted that each group used its own speed and so no two speeds were the same, and therefore no two "ideal" distances were the same.

Conclusion

Allowing children to work on a problem they have chosen for themselves confirms their ideas and actions. It validates them as learners. As a teacher, I have learned to recognize that their developing ideas are part of those larger concepts. Their developing ideas are just as important as the accepted scientific ideas. As we look at the evidence and consider it, our ideas shift. Over the course of several explorations and on into the phase of investigation, we are putting the bits and pieces together into larger concepts. The language in the early explorations is fairly simple compared to the language used at the level of investigation.

When sustaining science activity in the form of exploration and investigation the way we do, there comes a point when I become so involved that I stop referring to "you" and "yours" and start saying "we" and "ours." Other than the preliminary exploration I did with the materials before starting our inquiry into waves, and the reading in activity books, curriculum guides, and Hewitt's *Conceptual Physics*, I had not done more than the introductory work myself. As a group we were putting the bits and pieces together into the larger concepts. Something very special happens during those moments when we are all learning together.

Chapter Six

Balls in Motion
We Could Make History with This!

Helen Kitchel

The room is filled with the sounds of balls skittering to a stop on the floor, hitting each other, and bouncing off the baseboard. There is lively talking going on. "Look, your ball made mine move!" "Hold it higher." "They're not the same." "Now it's your turn. I'll watch." "We're going to find out if a ball's heavier, will it go faster? We could make history with this!" Two girls are putting balls in balance pans. Kids are everywhere in the room—talking, moving things, writing on clipboards. These second graders are doing an initial exploration of balls in motion.

Usually I am moving quickly around the room to watch each group work and ask a few questions while keeping an eye on other groups. But today I allow myself a few extra seconds to stay back and watch the whole scene of children actively engaged in carrying out their own explorations. I feel alone in this noisy, busy, seemingly chaos-filled classroom, watching nineteen seven-year-old scientists hard at work. I know that this is a scene of good science teaching and learning. I now trust my own instincts in organizing effective classroom activity in this field. But, good science learning did not happen by chance. It comes after many teacher planning sessions and previous discussions with the children about work sessions. It also comes when I let the students take some control over their learning.

Making a Start

I start with the district curriculum. Motion/Forces is one of four required units of study in physical science at the first- and second-grade level. To get an idea of what students at this age can do and think, I check national and state standards. Science activity books help me expand my background on the subject as I plan focused explorations and gather ideas for possible materials to use.

Next, I do some hands-on exploring with my teaching colleague, Jody Hall. It helps to think about the materials out loud with someone else. We gather up related materials scrounged from around the school—a collection of balls of varied material, size, and weight, and a collection of toy cars and ramps. We play and talk. We get an idea of what might happen when our students put their hands on the same materials. We try to connect what the curriculum guidelines say about forces with what we're noticing and what we think kids can do. For adults, exploration quickly leads to investigation, but I know children need more time for exploration. Working with the materials and equipment myself brings a new energy to the process. It makes me feel more connected to the students and their work. I find that ideas about which materials to have available for children and how to organize their distribution surface during this teacher play time.

First Thoughts About Motion

Getting at children's own ideas about a topic is very important because their ideas influence what they can do and know. I record their ideas about forces and motion on an overhead projector.

Children's ideas have value. I am careful to record them in their language, but at the same time I listen closely for the language of *pushing, pulling, stopping, starting,* and *changing motion.* Although gravity may be a somewhat higher concept, I listen for that, too, since it will become important later in elementary school.

In the first session I ask the children, "What are your ideas about moving things?" Many hands go up. Some name things that move. I direct them to describe how things move. I record their responses:

> animals move—muscles; cars move; people walking; people move by
> blood pumping to muscles—they get warmed up; bones help you to
> move; joints in fingers; wind and ocean move; clouds move; earth
> moves; airplanes move; heart beats; body parts move; things at-
> tached to body move when you move; planets move; kick dirt to

make it move; wind makes things move; rain moves; clothes in the washer move; toy robots move with battery wires; force of waves moves things on the beach; Slinky moves—hold in hand, vibrates.

The brainstorming gets off to a slow start, as it often does. One boy's association with the question about moving things leads to a discussion of insects:

Student: The way insects move they need sense.

Helen: OK. Keep talking.

Student: Ants have to be very careful about moving. I've got a bug collection. Ants are hard to catch. They could smell my sense and they will move.

Helen: Why do you think they will move?

Student: They move by the sense of their smell.

Helen: How would they move?

Student: They'd fly away.

Helen: So they would move by flying.

At this point I ask, "Are insects the only things that move?" I want to maintain the focus on movement and at the same time widen the range of moving things. When students name something, I prompt them to say something about how it moves:

Student: Planets move.

Helen: What do you mean planets move?

Student: They go around a circle around the sun.

Helen: What makes them move?

Student: Gravity.

In this next instance I introduce the term *pushes,* and a student echoes it. This is a term I know we will begin to develop in the next session.

Student: Plants are moved by the wind.

Helen: How does a plant move when it sprouts and pushes up? How does it move up through the ground?

Student: A seed pushes its way up.

These exchanges show how I find out what the children are thinking.

I want to narrow our study of moving things to the forces of pushing and pulling. In our next session I show a transparency of an outdoor scene—several children are engaged in outdoor activities involving motion and forces, as well as natural forces such as wind and water in motion. A visual cue is especially important for a number of my students. The overhead is a great success. I say, "Tell me about some motion you see in the picture." I question them further about pushing and pulling involved in the picture they are describing. I expect them to notice that pushing and pulling go together. For example, as the boy climbs the tree, he pulls with his arm on the rung above while pushing with his feet. The children also come up with several observations that I have not noticed, such as the girl's skirt being pushed by the wind.

From the beginning of this discussion I prompt the students by asking, "Is that pushing and pulling?" Pushing and pulling link forces with motion. Immediately students begin to use this language:

Wind is pushing the grass and flowers.

[The child is] pulling arms to move on roller skates.

The wind is blowing and pushing the sailboat.

The hill and gravity are making the waterfall move.

A child is using muscles to push and pull to climb a tree.

As the students make their observations, I label the images with the terms *pushing* and *pulling*. In this way I link forces with motion.

I am amazed at how a simple picture can elicit so many significant responses from the students. It is exciting to hear them talk more specifically and thoughtfully about forces. This feels like important work!

A variation is to have the children draw their own scene, after the brainstorming, of moving things that could then be labeled and discussed later. Photos of the playground during recess would also demonstrate forces and motion.

Exploring Forces on the Playground

Working on our school playground seems like the next logical step. It's a vast castlelike structure of ramps, climbing apparatuses, bars for hanging and climbing, swinging tires, balance beams, bridges, tunnels, stairs, ladders, and monkey bars. There are lots of pushing and pulling opportunities. Most important, it's theirs. Here we can connect classroom learning with the real world.

I bring the children together and explain that we will be going outside to our playground to see if they can learn more about force and motion with the equipment there. Managing the group outside the classroom is challenging. In fact, I must admit that there are times when I would rather not do it! Therefore, I start this activity inside by asking the children what they could do to work seriously, safely, and happily on the playground. We role play what our working behavior will look like once we do get outside on the equipment.

Outside, the children work with partners, making their observations on recording sheets attached to clipboards. Half the recording sheets say, "Find places where you start movement by pushing," and the other half say, "Find places where you start movement by pulling." Since we are the only group out on the playground, it is relatively quiet, and much to my relief a worklike atmosphere prevails. Partners fan out into all parts of the playground.

At the "hanging triangles," I ask Ned what he's noticing. Immediately he pushes a triangle with his hand and says, "You push it to make it move." While demonstrating, he says he's hanging from the triangles. "You pull on it when you hang from it."

"What are you noticing?" I ask Catty as she climbs up a cube structure of Goodyear tires. "You have to pull onto this," she says. On the swinging balance beam she says, "You can push down on one end and the other end goes up."

Julie says, "I pull on the chain and it moves," and Katie notes, "I pull the handles, and I go up the stairs."

This session goes especially well considering it is the first time we are using the playground for science work. Even those who cannot resist playing are still focused on their task when questioned by an adult. At the end of the playground session I gather the group together for a brief discussion of what they noticed.

On another day class members share the observations they have recorded on their clipboards and then make diagrams of what they found out. At my suggestion, a few students use labels and arrows that show action. Christian shares a detailed drawing that shows how his body moved (Figure 6–1). Emily's diagrams of swinging are labeled *push* or *pull* (Figure 6–2). Discussing ways to show more in a diagram would make a good minilesson before another session. From these diagrams we make a class mural of "Forces at Work on Kidspace."

Making diagrams and sharing them are ways for kids to communicate, an important science process skill. The whole-class discussion teaches the students that their recordings and diagrams have the purpose of organizing their findings to share with others. They learn that others have different approaches and observations. I encourage them to think more carefully about their work and what further questions they may have about it.

At this point I could keep going with the playground work and do an investigation of, for example, "What playground objects require the most push power to move?" The children have had enough exploration to move in this direction. Playground work, however, is

Figure 6–1
Christian

Figure 6–2
You can pull when you swing.

challenging to manage, and the weather is undependable. In what follows I describe a unit on motion and forces that is more easily managed in the classroom—a study of balls.

Getting Ready to Explore Balls

Setting objects in motion appeals to children: They can immediately see the results of their actions. My own exploration of materials at hand has led me to choose the ball collection of various materials, sizes, and weights. We could study the toy cars, but I think that the relation of different-sized wheels to force and movement on ramps is too complex for second graders. Also, the fantasy world of cars might take an upper hand over scientific work. Another year my children and I studied force and motion by loading up empty checkbook boxes and sliding them down ramps, but I want to work with some new materials. I am hoping that the balls will allow children to explore and investigate forces at play in motion.

The day before we start work I ask everyone to bring in a ball the next day that we can use in our science investigation. I send a note home with each second grader:

> Please bring tomorrow: 1 or 2 balls no larger than a fist! We are studying motion and need balls for our exploration. We are looking for balls of different weights, sizes, and materials. Thank you for helping out!

An Initial Exploration with Balls

The children work in pairs. I ask them to "see what you can find out about the balls." I have marked off areas of the room with masking tape on the carpet or floor to set some limits on the initial exploration. Each pair uses their own balls brought in from home and, if they want, some from the classroom collection.

Balls are examined and properties are discussed. I hear a couple of girls use the terms *soft*, *hard*, and *springy*. Balls are on the move! They bounce off the floor and walls; they roll on the linoleum, carpet, or table; they drop, rise, and hit other balls. Elizabeth spends most of the time lightly bouncing a group of balls on the table and watching them stop.

As the children work, my role is to be an observer. I do not want to be directly involved with their work at this time, because I need to convey the message to them that they have a free hand to explore the materials the way they want—not the way I want. I concentrate on taking notes on what I see and hear. These notes will help me to direct future activity. Occasionally, however, I do ask open-ended questions such as "What are you trying to find out?" Or "What else could you try?"

I hear Jack tell Mary that his golf ball didn't move at home, but it moves here! Mary tells him, "Maybe you have a wooden table at home that is rougher and keeps it from moving."

After ten minutes of this activity, I call the class together in our rug area and ask for volunteers to share their discoveries. Sharing early in the activity gives students other ideas for further work. I ask, "What did you notice about the balls?" A few hands are up instantly and the discussion begins. "Some bounce and some can't," is the first observation. "They are all round and roll on the floor—except the Koosh ball." Others mention such properties as size and color, and especially the materials from which the balls are made—steel, rubber, cloth, wood, plastic, metal. Others note that some can change their shape, and some are sticky, smooth, and bumpy. I have a brief exchange with a student about weight, which shows how I reinforce correct scientific terminology:

Student: Some balls are heavy and some are not.

Helen: So what do we call that?

Student: The weight.

Helen: The weight, right. Heavy or lightweight. That's right.

Weighing the balls on the balance becomes an area of interest for some of the children.

Second Exploration: More Focused and Sustained Work

After this sharing session of seven or eight minutes, the children go back to exploring for another ten minutes. Their observations are more refined and precise. I see the following:

Two students have different balls, which they are blowing across the floor with straws. They are very interested in getting the balls to roll in a straight line to the opposite side of the room.

One girl is rolling several balls into a corner and watching the action of each as it rebounds. Soon she shifts to bouncing them and counting how many bounces each ball goes before it stops.

Two boys are putting balls in order by weight. I get a balance and some washers to use for weighing.

Two students tell me they are trying to hit a ball with another one so that the first ball keeps going, but they can't make it work.

At the end of the session we briefly discuss the children's findings. The balances were popular. One student made an exciting discovery for himself about conservation:

Helen: Was it hard to use the scale? I noticed a lot of people learning how to use the scale. People were careful and really watching and counting how many things they were putting in and watching what they were doing. Anything else you want to say about the weight? What did you find about the weight of the balls? Jack, you did a lot of weighing.

Jack: Well, here was this big ball, like this one. And it weighed eighteen pounds—eighteen washers. Eighteen washers. And there was another one like this, except a lot *bigger*, and it weighed only fifteen washers!

Some are only at the exploring stage, while others are already raising investigation questions and trying to answer them, like the boys dropping balls and comparing the relation between weight and speed of the drop.

Next I move to a sorting activity with our large collection of balls. Sorting is an excellent way to get children to make finer observations. It calls attention to special properties of the balls that affect their movement, and it helps the children refine their science vocabulary. Following the sorting the children write and make a diagram about something important that they have discovered so far in their explorations with balls. They eagerly set about putting their thoughts down on paper. Here are a few examples:

When I bounced them a little they rold around but when I laft them alon they dident role.

[Dictated to me] We found out that some balls bounce and some balls don't.

I trid seeing what ball can bows the hoiest. [This student included a wonderful drawing with an arrow pointing up beside the ball's trajectory, and motion marks—like cat's whiskers—rising from the point on the floor where the ball changed direction.]

Another student created a detailed drawing of balls ordered by size.

Second graders are capable of communicating a great deal to each other during exploration and discussion, and I think they learn a great deal from each other and from my coaching. For these reasons I give them much more time to do that kind of work than to write and make diagrams.

Discussion of Drawings

The next day we start in a large group by sharing drawings made after yesterday's work. They are eager to share! We sit in a circle. I have paper on an easel and a clipboard with paper. I want to get good notes, and it is sometimes hard to write on easel paper while watching the class.

Discussion that comes after a few explorations and time for reflection is probably the most exciting moment for me as a teacher. The children and I have all had some experiences with the materials and have "talked the talk" enough to have a common vocabulary and awareness of the problems inherent in the materials. The discussion is rich, deep, and sustained. We are on the same wavelength. The following exchanges show what is possible when science is sustained.

In the first instance, a student presents his drawing depicting his work at the balance. He is the student who had earlier found out—much to his amazement—that a big ball can be lighter than a small ball. This exchange shows how I act as a coach to help students clarify their explanation of their work:

Helen: What are you trying to find out?

Student: I'm trying to find out if the one would weigh more than the metal one, than the small one.

Helen: All right. What was this one called? [I point to the large ball in the drawing.]

Student: Plastic.

Helen: You had a plastic ball, and you had a metal ball. Can you tell us the question you were trying to answer?

Student: Well, I was trying to find out 'cause the little ball was a silver one, and I wanted to see if the big plastic balls would weigh more.

Helen: Oh, so your question was, "Is the metal ball heavier than the plastic one?" And what did you find out?

Student: I found out that the metal one was heavier.

Helen: Did you think that the metal one was going to be heavier before you weighed them? Did you make a prediction?

Student: I thought it was going to weigh more. Now I know that the little balls that are made of metal weigh more than the plastic ones.

Another pair of students explored stopping and starting move-ment and changing direction by blowing on marbles with straws. In what follows, their initial verbalization of what happened is sketchy, similar to the student in the previous example. By probing I am able to get them to explain what happened in more precise terms and call everyone's attention to the starting, stopping, and changing-direction aspects of motion and force. I am able to do this because of my famil-iarity with recent curriculum frameworks that outline these impor-tant concepts in this area of science.

Student: We tried two marbles and when they hit each they both went . . . and then came back and went around in a circle . . . and then they went way down and went boom.

Helen: How many times did you get them started?

Student: Three times.

Helen: Let's draw a diagram of that. Here's a marble and here's a marble. Did Katie hit one and you hit the other? Did you hit it with your pencil?

Student: No, we blew on it.

Helen: Great! You blew on them to get them going. Oh boy, this is a great di-agram. OK. And then this one went this way, and this one went this way. And what happened here?

Student: They both went ka-pooie.

Helen: Could you use a more scientific word for *ka-pooie?* Did they hit each other? OK. They hit each other. This one went this way and this one went that way? So your diagram could show when they hit and then what hap-pened after they hit, with arrows showing the direction the balls moved in. What made them stop?

Student: The thing that made them stop is when they both hit, they went separate ways.

Helen: Then did they keep on going?

Student: They went on the floor.

Helen: Did they start on the desk?

Student: Yes, then onto the floor.

Helen: And then what?

Student: They kept going and then they stopped. Catty stopped them.

Helen: How did Catty stop them?

Student: She put her foot on them.

Helen: Do you remember what happened when the marble touched her foot?

Student: Yeah, it stopped.

Helen: What do you think made them keep going when they went off the desk onto the floor? Any ideas? Why did they keep going?

Student: Because of the force of what they hit.

Helen: Great. What keeps them going? The force of the hit back there. Alright, you're thinking.

I try to underscore key concepts with my questioning. I realize I could also direct their attention to the pull of gravity and the force generated when the ball hit the ground, but gravity is out of sight, and perhaps too abstract at this point.

The final exchange deals with a boy whose notebook states that the Play-Doh held the ball. In this session he explains that they made a ball by placing a metal ball inside Play-Doh and "rolled it around and your couldn't see the ball but you could see the Play-Doh and it fell hard because the ball was inside it." After more discussion a girl suggests an explanation for why the Play-Doh went faster with the metal ball inside: "Once the metal ball turns once and it spins the rest, all of it is really heavy and Play-Doh is pretty light, so it didn't have anything to force it to turn the rest of the way to keep it going around. The metal ball does, so it can push down itself to make it move." This is very sophisticating thinking, which moves in the direction of Newton's laws. It is exciting to hear her thinking on this level. The beauty of this approach is that students can work side by side on very different levels.

This same girl often raises her hand. It's hard to avoid calling on her because she *always* has something interesting to say! Today her idea is especially interesting because it is "an existing idea, rather different from the accepted 'scientific' ones" (Harlen 1985a). She and Philip have been using the scales. They used two balls that she describes as "the same." I ask her to tell us more about how they are the same. She replies, "They were exactly the same, made out of heavy metal. I put them on at the same time so they weighed the same. I did it at the same time so it would be a fair test. I thought the last one on would weigh more." I carry the scale over to the table so I can demonstrate what she means to the class. She cautions me about how I should put things onto the scale. I explain to the class that this might be a good question for investigation: "Does the way you put things on a scale affect their weight?" Later she works with another girl on this problem for about five minutes.

Only five children share. I am watching the clock and know that we have to get going on the hands-on work. The kids are getting restless. We discuss the proper use of the balance and I show them the catalogue and how much balances cost. They still love to "load 'em up"!

It is time for another brief exploration. Sarah and Jane complain that Justin is not sharing the balance. It's a good opportunity to explain why partners can be helpful observers while someone else takes a turn. A few students have difficulty working with others, but they do have ideas to explore. One girl is testing two balls to see how high they bounce. I suggest that her partner watch her and record the results. By this time two girls, who have been exploring the problem of weighing balls in the balance pans are blowing marbles across the table. The boy who reported on the Play-Doh ball continues his exploration with the same materials.

Building a Bridge to Investigation

Different themes have emerged from the children's work: the effects of bouncing balls, weight, blowing as a force, and the effects of one ball hitting another. Jody and I frame a question that is a bridge to investigation: "What do you notice when you bounce different balls on the floor?" I put them into pairs and each pair selects five balls to work with.

Students immediately set to work on the problem. There is a sense of purposeful activity and a strong command of a language to describe what is going on. One student tells me excitedly, "We had a tennis ball and a bouncy ball. The bouncy ball went higher up. We tried it lower and the bouncy ball still went higher." I notice another pair has finished bouncing the balls, and I suggest that they order them from least to most bouncy. Two girls want to explain their finding to me. I suggest that they make a diagram of what they did. I comment favorably on a pair who are taking great care in making the balls drop from the same height. One boy says to another, "The big metal ball didn't go as high as the little metal ball." Philip explains how he eliminated the bouncy ball from his work since it was so obvious to him that it would always bounce higher than others.

At this point it is important to note that our ball collection contained a wide variety of balls of different materials and sizes. Given the materials, it was almost impossible to control variables and do fair tests, because there were no sets of three balls of the same material and different size, nor were there sets of balls of the same size and different material. This is not good for investigation because it is impossible to make fair tests unless all but one variable is kept the same. In the existing ball situation we could make a beginning effort at investigating the effect of weight or material on bounce. We did have a small number of metal balls in two sizes, but not enough for the entire class. Nevertheless, we went ahead, trusting that these kinds of lessons can come up in the work of investigation and that science is the process of raising questions and learning about what the variables are and what needs to be done to control them.

Planning for Investigation: Which Ball Will Bounce the Highest?

The next day's work involves writing plans for investigation. There will be no hands-on work, but I feel the class is ready to work in this fashion. The children have really come along in their ability to work together. We read the question together: "Which ball will bounce the highest?" Then we discuss the worksheet. I explain that each group will have three balls with which to work: a very light one, a medium-weight one, and a heavy one. I tell them that they have made good progress in thinking like scientists. We go over my expectations for what they write on their plan: the question, the names of children in the group, their prediction, and a plan that includes information about how they will measure. Figures 6–3 and 6–4 show two plans.

Figure 6–3
Investigation Plan

Investigation Plan

Our group: Joel Eric Olivia

Question: Which ball bounces the highest?

Predictions: I think the lightest ball will bounces the highest.

Plan:

Eric drops balls, Joel + Olivia watch.

ruler

Eric

Figure 6–4
Investigation Plan

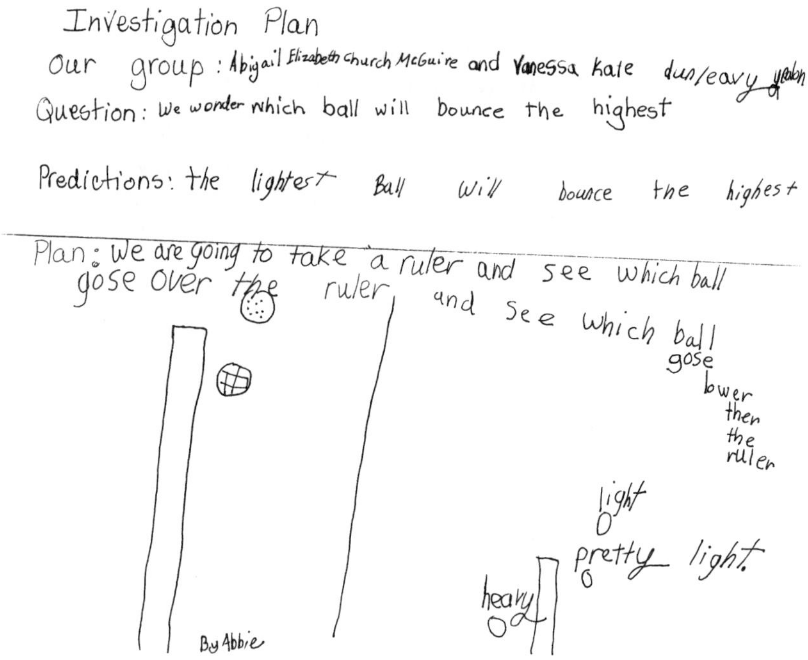

Investigation Plan
Our group: Abigail Elizabeth Church McGuire and Vanessa Kate dun/eavy yohn
Question: We wonder which ball will bounce the highest

Predictions: the lightest Ball will bounce the highest

Plan: We are going to take a ruler and see which ball
gose over the ruler, and see which ball gose
lower then the ruler

light
pretty light.
heavy

By Abbie

Investigation

Before launching into the actual investigations, groups share their plans with each other. One group reads their plan: "Some of the light balls bounce the same as the heavy balls. We will hold them at the same height and drop them. We will take turns." When I ask these students why they plan to hold the balls at the same height, they tell me that one ball at one height and one at a lower height would not be a fair test. They continue, "The very light ball will bounce higher. We are going to take a yardstick and bounce the balls. We're going to try a lot of times to be exact." The plans reveal that measurement is either by ruler, hands, or eyes. I say it is all right to measure in different ways.

I next ask, "What about the way the ball is dropped? Would it be OK to have one ball dropped and one that you push down with your hand?" There are several responses: "If you give it a lot of force it will bounce high." "It will give it a lot more speed then it will bounce too high. It won't be a fair test." "If you push it down, it will hit the ground harder and it will bounce higher." "If you pushed it, it would go higher."

Groups fan out over the room and the work begins. In the investigation Jody and I busy ourselves coaching the students in the skills of repeating tests, making measurements, and writing up the results. One student seems quite baffled that the balls all bounce the same height despite their weight. I ask him to try again and have his partner watch the outcome. She reports: "The heavy ball hardly bounced." He sees it and hears her comment, but I am still not sure he believes it! Three students find out that the very light ball bounces the highest, the medium-weight ball the second highest, and the metal one the lowest. I ask them how they found out. They say they dropped them at the same time. While one person dropped the balls, the others watched closely for the height of the bounce. Another group has similar results; their report includes a chart of the weight of each ball in terms of washers in the balance pan and measurements for heights. Another group makes a diagram of balls bouncing up off the floor, with lines representing the height of each ball.

In our last discussion about balls we talk about why light balls bounce higher than heavy balls. One student says, "The small one is so light it bounces high; the heavy one is so heavy it just drops to the ground." Another says, "Because the heavy one doesn't pull itself down." An important exchange about the effect of weight and kind of material on bounce occurs. One student says, "I tried a big glass marble and a very small metal ball. The glass ball went higher. It was heavier. I wondered if weight had anything to do with how high it bounces." Another student notes, "Rubber bounces and metal does too, but it only bounces an inch high." I ask, "Why do you think that is so?" The student replies, "Because rubber has something bouncy." Another student adds, "Because metal is heavier than rubber. There's a force pulling the ball down. Metal balls are heavy." This leads another student to say, "Some of the light balls will bounce the same as the heavier balls." I ask, "Why do you think that happens?" She replies, "Some balls are bouncy." Another adds, "The very light ball will bounce higher. I don't think the heavy ball will bounce that much."

Reflection on the Teaching of Science

I feel good about my work as a teacher of science. The students have come a long way in terms of staying focused during exploration. What looked like play at the beginning takes on the look of real work. My notes from one of the later explorations say, "I was comfortable with the level of activity." What in the beginning felt like organized chaos seems highly directed. The children have grown into the scientific process. I have grown as a facilitator and observer. Working with colleagues in a study group and with a teaching colleague, Jody Hall, has helped keep all the work on a high level—always moving forward and always purposeful. I feel comfortable leading the class through discussions. My time spent on reflecting about their earlier work, drawings, and comments has paid off! I have given them enough time to explore their materials. In leading the discussion, I ask questions that support their specific observations, help them think more clearly about their findings, and lead them on to further questions. The comments of the children make sense and are more precise as we extend our work with the balls. The seriousness the children have developed regarding their work is a result, I believe, of my giving them enough time for exploration and of my listening respectfully to them. The discussion feels authentic and valuable. It is exhilarating to realize that it all comes from my own thinking rather than from a teacher's manual! The students went beyond the expectations I had at the very beginning in terms of sustaining this kind of work.

Chapter Seven

Learning About Light

Pedie O'Brien

Light is an area of study for fourth graders in our school. The National Research Council (1996) standards state that by fourth grade children should learn that, "Light travels in a straight line until it strikes an object. Light can be reflected by a mirror, refracted by a lens, or absorbed by the object."

Science in the National Curriculum (DES 1989) suggests that children can learn about several properties of light. Between the ages of seven and eleven they should:

- know that light passes through some materials and not others, and that when it does not, shadows may be formed
- be able to draw pictures, showing features such as light, color, and shade
- know that light can be made to change direction and shiny surfaces can form images
- be able to give an account of an investigation with mirrors
- know that we see objects because light is scattered off them and into our eyes
- know that light travels in straight lines and use this to explain the shapes and sizes of shadows
- understand how light is reflected

In our study of light we cover some but not all of these ideas.

My teaching colleague, Jody Hall, and I met briefly throughout the unit to plan and assess the work. Because of our common framework, which includes five years of working together doing action research to learn this approach, minimum contact was required to make what follows happen.

Whenever I begin a unit, I start by brainstorming with the students to see what they know about the subject. Here are some of the ideas about light expressed by my fourth graders:

It makes the world bright.

Makes heat.

Reflects off shiny things.

Helps you see.

Makes you grow.

Wakes you up.

Makes pictures come out.

Can be natural like the sun or man-made like a flashlight.

Makes shadows.

Makes the room bright.

Part of making a rainbow.

Makes leaves on trees in the spring.

Burns things like the sun. Fire.

Evaporates water.

Can make optical illusions.

It is apparent that some students are using the same language as the curriculum guidelines—for example, that light makes shadows, reflects off shiny things, can be natural or man-made, and is part of making a rainbow.

After the brainstorming session I do another preassessment by giving them this picture showing the sun, a tree, and a person. I ask them to make a picture into a diagram by using arrows to show how the person can see the tree, and to write a short comment about it. The arrows are supposed to show the direction the light is traveling in. Their responses fall into three categories:

1. Ten children think that a straight line of light beams from the person's eyes to the tree, enabling the person to see. The diagrams show lines of light beaming from the person's eyes to the tree.

2. Two children think that light is shining on everything and at the same time that light is emanating from the eye, as an independent light source like a flashlight.

3. No one understands that light reflects on the tree and travels to the person's eyes.

Here are sample comments concerning the first response:

He can see the tree with his eyes. The sun gives him Light to see it better.

The person can see the tree becuse the sun is helping him see it.

When the light shines down on us and the tree your eyes can see lot's of things like a tree.

This comment was part of the second response:

the sun is shining on the shinny Leaves and Bouncing of on to the Boys eyes then the Beam of Light Bounced off the Boys eyes and Back on to the tree again.

First Exploration: Pocket Mirrors and a Flashlight

We start the first exploration with the invitation, "See what you can find out using pocket mirrors and a flashlight." Flashlights have instant appeal. Furthermore, they can be used to demonstrate that light travels in straight lines. Children explore two things: reflections in the mirrors without using the flashlights and reflections of light in a darkened room with mirrors. They have ten minutes to explore in a darkened room and ten minutes to explore in a bright room.

Jody Hall and I serve as facilitators, wandering to different groups to direct their attention to the possibilities with open-ended questions. While some teachers in our study group prefer to say little during explorations, I like to prompt students as they work. Directing the question "What are you noticing?" to a group that is making relevant observations can cue others who are not sure how to explore light with the materials. Other kinds of questions stimulate activity: "How far can you make your reflection go?" "What happens when you reflect your light off the mirror?"

In the discussion about the flashlight exploration that follows the activity, one group reports that they put the mirror on the floor, aimed the flashlight "diagonally" on the mirror, and found that the light reflected on the ceiling. Another group found that they could redirect the beam of light anywhere in the room by tilting the mirror. The language of *beam of light* and *reflect* has caught on. Students note that putting something over half of the flashlight results in a reflection of half-beam. Others explain that two flashlights together make much brighter light than one by itself; when tested, the reflection on the ceiling was much brighter.

I find that students' language is often vague in the first explorations, and I need to model more precise terminology (in this case, the term *reflection*). One student says, "The reflection was like a bouncing ball; it went up and down like that." I ask her, "Could you describe what you had to do to your mirror to make it do that?" She replies, "I moved it, and it made it look like it was bouncing." I repeat this statement, modeling more precise language, "So you flipped the mirror back and forth, and it made the reflection look like it was bouncing."

One group reports that they reflected light from a wall mirror to their small hand-held mirror. This generates a lot of interest. Later Jody and I will structure the next exploration around this property of light.

Students explain that in the exploration with mirrors and no flashlights, they found that using a couple of mirrors held close to their eyes, like blinders on a horse, created the reflection of several faces; that holding up the mirror at an angle reflected other parts of the room; and that by using two mirrors they could see the back of their head. One student notes that when you look at a mirror with a highly scratched surface "from the diagonal view" you can see "double."

In the discussion I find that students get ideas from others for what they want to explore. So at the end of this brief discussion I allow enough time for students briefly to repeat the exploration. Then they record their observations in their notebooks. Here are a couple of their journal entries:

Expieriment With flashlight and Miror

This is one of the things I lernd today. I lernd that if you take two mirors and put one in from of your head and one in the back of your head you can see the back of your head.

Lights

When I put a mirior in front of my flash light it reflected off my mirior and you could see the light in a diferent spot.

I put two miriors on the side of my eyes and one on top and one on botom. You can see your face 1,000 times

The students have had a lot of fun, especially with the mirrors and flashlights, and they are anxious to work with light again.

A Game of "Pass the Light"

The next day, picking up on their interest in reflecting light off the mirrors, I give groups of five students four pocket mirrors and ask them to explore flashlight reflections in them. I explain, "See what happens when you explore with one flashlight and several mirrors." I want to give them some time to explore freely before asking them to do more directed work. After ten minutes of exploration and a brief discussion, I ask the students, "Can you make light from a flashlight reflect from four mirrors before hitting a target?" After more discussion about their observations during this activity, they make journal entries. I find that some students make pictures, some create diagrams, some use a mix of words and either pictures or diagrams, and some prefer to use words only. The following entry is indicative of the students' enthusiasm and reveals an important finding about the spacing of group members:

> Today we plays a game with flashlights and mirors. The game was you had 2 try to get the flashlight to reflet of the mirors and on to something. I thout it was really fun I think it is easyer when your group is closer to gether.

During discussion a lot of attention is given to how light travels, which brings about the next exploration. We are unable to find activities for this in our books, so we ask a physics teacher for ideas. He suggests that we beam a flashlight through chalk dust in a darkened room and through water filled with tiny suspended particles, like nondairy creamer, which will reflect the beam of light. (Please note that after we initiated the chalk-dust activity, we were alerted to the fact that the dust could endanger some children's health. Please do not repeat this activity.)

Exploring Beams of Light

The next day, Jody tells the children, "In order to help us understand what happens when light travels, Mrs. O'Brien and I are going to hold a couple of erasers and clap them so that there is some chalk dust in the air. That way we can see what happens when the light goes through the chalk dust. Before we do that, can you make a prediction about what will happen?" The students make three predictions about what the light will do: push the chalk dust down to the ground; make a little hole for the light to go through; and move right through the chalk dust. The first two predictions presume that light has a pushing force strong enough to move dust particles; the third prediction presumes that light will pass through the particles but it says nothing about reflecting off of them. After watching the effects of shining a light through the dust, students have these things to say:

Student: The chalk dust travels with light.

Student: When you shine your flashlight near the top, the chalk dust came over to the light.

Student: It lights up the whole thing.

Student: The chalk follows your flashlight.

Student: There was a round cloud of dust around the light in the flashlight.

Student: When you shine light through the chalk dust, the beam of light goes straight.

Student: When [the light is] in dust it seemed to go slower and near ground slower.

Student: The turned-on flashlight seemed to attract the dust.

Student: We should do it without the dust to see if it's brighter when there's nothing in the air.

Student: I noticed it was brighter where the dust was.

Teacher: Why do you think it was brighter where the dust was?

Student: Maybe the light was shining on the dust.

Student: It looks like dust is coming out of the flashlight. The beam of light is attracted to chalk.

Student: Light acts like a magnet.

Student: What is happening is that light is reflecting off of things.

Student: In a darkened room you can see the light going through the dust.

Student: Not all the light gets through.

Student: When the light falls on the dust particles, maybe they fall to the ground.

This is a wonderful set of observations. If the activity would not pose a danger, we might go on to investigate the hypotheses that light is brighter when it shines on dust, that chalk follows the light, or that the light attracted dust.

In the next exploration I give students flashlights and darken the room. Groups move from station to station, where aquariums of water are set up. Two aquariums contain clear water, two contain water to which a small amount of nondairy creamer has been added, and another contains water made very cloudy with the creamer. We ask students, "Look at flashlight beams in milky water and clear water. What do you notice?" Later, each group records their observations in their notebooks and on large sheets of paper:

Group 1

It goes through the murkiest water best. You can't see the beam of light very well through the clear water. The light makes the water a mirror. When you put the flashlight on the side it bounces of the other side?

Group 2

You can see threw the clear and the light water. You can see a beam of light threw the water. You can oly see a little light threw the darkest one. When you shine the light trew the clear and light water you can see a orang beam. When you shine the light in the darkest water you can see a beam. If you look threw the other side of the pal you can see a little orang spark. If you make a beam threw the clear water you can see the beam on the table and it will flicker.

Group 3

When you flash the light in the milky water it lights up most of the bowl. When you flash the light in the clear water it looks like the ground is up higher. The beam moves in the not so milky water and not in the really milky water. The flashlight lights up the whole bowl in the not so milky water and the really milky water.

Group 4

You put a flashlight on one side of the clear water and it goes thro the water the thro the other side and goes on an object on the other side. The milkiest water glows in the dark when the flashlights are off. You can see the beam of light easer in the milky water than you can in the clear water. If you shin a light in the clear water you can see the dust on the side it looks like stars.

During the discussion it is evident that the students are really thinking about the effects of light. They want to talk about the way the flashlight could light up the "whole bowl" of milky water. Someone suggests that the light "catches" on the tiny bits of milky stuff. Someone else says that light was reflecting on those bits, and that's why everything lit up. That suggestion is related to the beam's showing up in the milky water and the dusty air. The discussion prompts one student to state that light travels at a really fast speed, leading another student to comment on light traveling from the sun and lighting the earth: "You know how on the earth one half is day when the other half is dark? Well, to get to the other half, like it bounces for a day on the first half, then it bounces another day on the second half."

Another student says, "The sun is really big so the light goes through space and comes down and touches the earth . . . on one side because it's nighttime on the other side." But someone else states, "Well, it doesn't travel. The earth is moving around and the sun is still shining when the other half is dark and the other part moves around." Jody asks him, "How then does light get here?" He replies, "I don't know." "How then," she asks "do you think light gets to us, when a lightbulb turns on and it's bright all of a sudden? How do you think the light gets from there to here?"

"A lightbulb," he replies, "gives light."

Diagraming a Candle

The question of how light gets from one place to another leads to an exercise with candles, to help students in their thinking about light traveling in straight lines. To start, I ask them to describe what they think light is. Students say, "It's a beam of light that lights up darkness." "When you turn on a light it just travels the speed of light. Like up in the sky it beams up and you can see." "A reflection of the sun."

Next I say, "I'm going to draw light traveling in three ways. In each I am going to put in a light source." In one picture I draw a flashlight with light beaming out from the light source—the light rays fanning out from the end of the flashlight in straight lines. In another I show light fanning out from both ends of the flashlight, and in the third I show light dribbling out of the light source in squiggly lines that move in all directions, including back to the light source. I ask, "Which one do you think shows best how light travels?"

After a discussion, everyone seems to agree that "light travels straight" and that the first picture most accurately shows how light travels. Following this discussion we give each group a candle to observe, with these directions: "You have thirty seconds. When I turn the light on I want *one person* to blow the candle out. Then I would like you to get your journals out and go back to your seats and draw how light travels from a candle. After you've done that, go up to the rug and sit with your group." The drawings of the members of one group indicate a range of thinking: two show light emanating in straight lines in all directions from the candle, one shows light radiating up and fanning out like a flashlight, and one shows a candle with no rays and the statement the "light travels in a strait line. On a candle the light doesn't travel in a beam." The last two statements indicate lingering misconceptions.

Investigating the Absorption Property of Light

As a way of identifying a topic for investigation, we list what we have learned so far about light on the board. One student states that light is absorbed by certain materials more than other materials. We turn this hypothesis over to an investigation question, "Which material absorbs the most light?" Next we come up with some predictions. We decide that students will use a flashlight to test aluminum foil, white paper, and black paper. Later that day students write up a plan for their investigations, which includes the investigation question, a hypothesis, two or three sentences stating what they will do, a list of the materials, and a statement about how they will measure the reflections. All hypothesize that the black paper will absorb the most light. Most "measure" with their eyes, but a couple of groups beam the flashlight at an angle to the test material and move a white card further and further from the material until they can no longer see a reflection from the test material. The distances are measured and entered on a chart. All agree that dark paper absorbs the most light, followed by white paper, and then aluminum foil.

In retrospect, it might be better to choose materials that are not quite so obvious but still have a discernible difference in measured light. We might be able to make better connections to everyday life by considering car safety in terms of which color car is most visible on the highway (e.g., investigating reaction times to different colored objects at a distance). Such an investigation might have more meaning to the students.

Conclusion

At the end of the unit we ask students to repeat the opening exercise: "Show how the eyes can see a tree by diagraming the flow of light in the picture of the sun, tree, and person." Because of scheduling, more children were able to do the exercise the second time around. Here are the results:

1. Two children think that light reflects off people's eyes so they can see the tree. A ray of light comes from the sun to the eyes, and finally to the tree.

2. Seven children think that light from the sun is shining on the person and the tree, but there is a lingering idea of the eye as an independent light source. In each diagram, a light ray with an arrow goes from the tree to the person's eyes, and a ray with an arrow goes from the eyes to the tree.

3. Ten children think that light rays from the sun shine on everything and are reflected in the person's eyes.

This comment is typical of the first reponse:

> The sun refexes off are eyes and hits the tree wicth you can see the tree.

These comments are meant to support the second response:

The suns light hits the tree bounces off and allows the boy to see out of his pupul.

Th sun is going to the teer and bosing of to the prsin so he can see

The way you would see the tree is the sun shines on the tree and tree reflects so you can see it [the tree].

Some of the students who had the third response wrote:

The light shines on the tree and it reflects on to the boy.

The boy sees the tree because the sun hits the tree and the light bounces of the tree to the boy's eye's.

A comparison of the results from the pre- and postassessment indicate that our classroom work led to growth in the students' thinking about light. Twelve students did the preassessment at the beginning of the unit, at which time ten students thought that light beamed like a

Figure 7–1
When the light shines down on us and the tree your eyes can see lot's of things like a tree.

and When the light shines down on us
and the tree your eyes can see lot's of
things like a tree.   Forrest

flashlight from the person's eyes; two thought that light bounced off the tree to the person, and at the same time thought of the eyes as a kind of flashlight. Nobody had the correct idea that light rays from the sun reflect off the tree to the person. Nineteen students did the postassessment. Three (only one of whom did the preassessment) thought that the eyes operate like a "flashlight"; seven thought that light shines everywhere and that the eyes are like a "flashlight"; eleven thought that rays of light travel in straight lines from the sun to the tree to the eyes.

The shift in thinking is best illustrated by making a comparison of a child's diagrams before and after the unit. Forrest shows a marked change from a view of the eye as a light source (Figure 7–1) to a view of rays of light reflecting off the surface of the tree, some of which reaches the eyes and enables that person to see the tree (Figure 7–2).

Teaching science with our model gives children the much-needed exploration—or what we might call "play"—that helps them understand science. This form of activity is not always accepted as worthwhile. Early in our work together we decided to secretly tape record a

Figure 7–2
The light shines on the tree and it reflects onto the boy.

group doing an exploration in the corner. Based on mere observation, Jody and I both thought they had spent most of the time just fooling around. To our surprise, when we listened to the tape we found that their observations were abundant and relevant to the topic. Given the opportunity, children will construct knowledge and gain skills in learning about the natural world. It isn't usually a quiet time, and it may even seem chaotic for the first few times, but we learned that if we could concentrate on being active listeners and watchers and learners with the children, we were amazed at how much they are actually learning.

Chapter Eight

Moving from Exploration to Investigation

Pat Pierce

A teacher who is beginning to use our approach may have difficulty with the transition from exploration to the more focused phase of investigation. The transition is difficult because teachers have to recognize what leads to fair testing and what does not. In addition, teachers must take their cues from the children and not attempt to rush the experience. Children need many opportunities to explore before they investigate. This can be difficult for those of us who are naturally fast paced and accustomed to directing every step of children's learning.

Investigation problems arise in explorations as children raise questions and generate ideas. The teacher observes the children carefully, always listening for suggestions of fair-testing kinds of problems in what the children do and say. It is essential for teachers to expose children to a wide variety of materials and experiences in the phase of exploration. This chapter shows how I managed a transition from exploration to investigation in a study of forces with my fourth and fifth graders. I describe children's ideas and questions about forces, which were generated in several explorations. I show how I reworked these comments into investigation problems.

One sunny fall day I took my class to the playground to explore forces. I asked them, "What do you notice about the forces of pushing and pulling when you use the playground equipment?" As I circulated among the groups, I recorded these comments:

I had to pull to get up those monkey bars.

I think the force [on the monkey bars] is from one hand to the other. Now [going up the ramp] it's my legs.

Across the bars, gravity is pulling you down, so you must have strength to pull up.

You have to pull [to get up the slide]. I like doing things with my arms 'cause I'm strong.

These children were starting to formulate hypotheses about forces. They were expressing their ideas and using words associated with forces, such as *pulling* and *pushing*, *starting* and *stopping*, and *gravity*.

While the children explore a science topic, I often ask them to record their observations in written form directly in a journal or on a loose sheet of paper attached to a clipboard. During a second playground exploration, the children observed forces of pushing and pulling and of starting and stopping. They recorded the following comments:

Clatter bridge—it is being pulled down when people walk on it.

When people go on [the clatter bridge] there is a lot of pressure.

When you go on the glider, you push off to start and then you jerk to a stop when you hit the end. Also, when you jump off, it makes a hole in the ground.

Tire ramp—force on legs.

Gravity is pulling you down so you have to have the strength to hold yourself up. When gravity is pulling you, you have to swing across.

When they land after they go through the tube slide, their feet make the hole bigger.

Following this playground exploration, I asked each child to divide a sheet of paper in half and diagram starting and stopping on a specific piece of playground equipment. As a class we had discussed the difference between drawings and diagrams and the importance of labeling in diagraming. The children had also shared different ways in which they could show movement and illustrate the direction and speed of this movement. Diagraming provides a vehicle for the children to move from active, hands-on learning to more abstract discussion and thought about their work.

Their diagrams reflected a range of ideas. Emily's diagram (Figure 8–1) indicated an understanding that jumping up to the monkey bars is pushing. Zac illustrated running by showing his figure leaning forward and pushing against the ground with his foot to start, and again push-

Figure 8–1
Emily

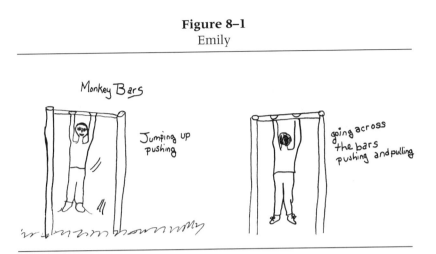

ing against the ground and leaning back as balance to stop (Figure 8–2). Kurt showed the direction of the turn on the tire swing and its relation to the pushing action of the feet (Figure 8–3). Anna drew the tire ramp and showed climbing it as an act of stopping and starting, and of pushing with your feet and pulling with your hands (Figure 8–4).

After another exploration, in which children explored forces at work in tug-of-war contests, I asked them to note questions and ideas for further work with forces:

"Mrs. Pierce, what is friction. I don't quite understand it."

"I would like to know why friction is caused by rubbing things together."

"Do we always slide on tile? If your shoes don't have a lot of tread, why don't they slide on a rug?"

"When we both pulled [in a tug-of-war], why didn't we just slip when we were in the lunchroom? I mean I know we were bracing our bodies so we didn't go head over heads but if we were both pulling and if we were each as strong wouldn't this happen?"

The first student wanted the teacher to give her an explanation of friction. The second knew what causes friction and wanted to know why it happens. She had the seeds of a hypothesis forming in her mind. The third student's question included a fair-testing possibility: he was wondering about variables that might create a difference in sliding. The fourth student was also beginning to move into the investigation phase with her questions about rope pulling and what makes the difference.

Figure 8–2
Running

Follow-up discussion is essential to the success of this approach. In my classroom I have found that discussions held immediately after activities are often disjointed and overly concrete. Children struggle to find the vocabulary to describe their experiences and often revert to hand motions. Many times they jump up, get the materials, and give spontaneous demonstrations to illustrate a point. I sometimes find that when a delay occurs between the exploration and the discussion, children seem able to operate better in the abstract and articulate their experiences using higher-level reasoning and vocabulary. It is almost as if they are too close to the experience initially to discuss it.

In the next session we held a class discussion about forces. Students were able to refine their questions. Jessica spoke about how slippery the lunchroom floor seemed when she did the rope pull. Later in the discussion she asked, "Why do tile floors make you slip and slide?"

Scott pointed out, "Norman and Carl are both the same size and both had on the same shoes. But Carl is built more and stronger. It depends on more strength."

Figure 8–3
Kurt

Nathan stated that he had "a lot better traction on the rug," and Kurt asked, "Do we always slide on tile?"

Finally, Sarah asked, just as she had in her journal, "I know what traction is, but what is friction?"

Later the class discussed an exploration with matchboxes. Two students had started and stopped matchboxes on different surfaces and with different weights. Erin and Jay noticed that the matchbox went slower on rough surfaces and wouldn't go at all with cloth on the board "unless we gave it a push." When talking about the effect of adding clay to the matchbox to weight it, another student commented that "at first the one with clay went fast, but with too much clay it will slow down."

These questions and hypotheses are the stepping stones that lead into the next phase of planning investigations. *It is essential that the teacher keep a careful record of the class discussions that follow exploration.* During these discussions children articulate questions and ideas that may be explored or investigated. Gradually, the ideas become more refined. I often keep a tape recorder running during a discussion. But

Figure 8–4
Tire Ramp

it can take long hours of transcribing to get to the critical material on the tape. It is most helpful if an experienced observer is available to record. Then the teacher can return to the taped version to fill in the details. Realistically, however, the classroom teacher seldom has such an observer available and must learn to lead the discussion and take notes simultaneously. This has been a difficult skill for me to master. With experience in inquiry science, however, I have learned to focus quickly on five or six productive comments that arise in a discussion. I record them in my notebook whenever I hear them. Written notes are necessary in this approach.

Learning to identify fair-testing problems in the children's comments is a major challenge for the teacher in the beginning. This is a good opportunity for two teachers to team and work together. While one leads the discussion, the other can take notes. As I was learning this approach, Jody Hall observed my classroom discussions on forces and kept a verbatim record of children's questions and comments. Later she and I studied her notes. We looked for evidence of investigation questions. We asked ourselves, "Which of these comments and

Figure 8–5
Comments and Questions

Comments and Questions	Possible Investigations
Sam: Norman and Carl are the same size, had on shoes with the same tread, and were both standing on the rug, but Carl pulled Norman across the room. Carl must be stronger than Norman.	In a rope pull, if two people are the same size and weight, and have on the same shoes, does strength make a difference? Plan an investigation to prove it.
Jessica: The lunchroom floor was real slippery during the rope pull. Why do tile floors make you slip and slide? Nathan: I had a lot better traction on the rug. Kurt: Do we always slide on tile? Sarah: I know what traction is, but what is friction?	Plan an investigation to determine the best surface for a tug-of-war.
Elena and Jayson: The matchbox went slower on rough surfaces, and it wouldn't go at all with cloth on the board unless we gave it a push.	Plan an investigation to find out what materials make the fastest surface for matchboxes to slide down.
Sarah: When we added clay to the matchboxes at first the one with clay went fast, but with too much clay, it will slow down.	Plan an investigation to determine the best amount of weight to make a matchbox go fastest down a ramp.

questions lead to fair testing? Which of these comments are hypotheses that can be tested?"

In the beginning I found it helpful to work with other teachers to search for comments that would move children toward investigation. In our study group we looked over children's work and identified promising observations and questions. Figure 8–5 illustrates how I reworked specific comments and questions into problems for investigation. Learning to rework children's observations, hypotheses, and questions is not an easy process, but as teacher and students become more comfortable with it, the transition from exploration to investigation happens with greater ease.

A neophyte to this approach might ask, "Wouldn't it be easier if I just made up the questions?" I have come to believe that at all times the investigations must arise from the children's own ideas and questions, not from those of the teacher. My experiences with my fourth and fifth graders have shown that the questions will arise, and children will move naturally into planning investigations when the atmosphere in the classroom encourages this direction. I have learned that the transition cannot be rushed. Children need many opportunities to explore. They need many opportunities to discuss their observations, to question their observations, and to think critically about them before moving into investigation.

Epilogue

If the intellectual powers are to develop, the child must gain a measure of control over his own thinking and he cannot control it while he remains unaware of it. The attaining of this control means prising thought out of its primitive unconscious embeddedness in the immediacies of living in the world and interacting with other human beings. It means learning to move beyond the bonds of human sense. It is on this movement that all the higher intellectual skills depend.

Margaret Donaldson,
Children's Minds

Moving Beyond Sense

Children gain intellectual powers as they explore the natural world and express their ideas. Over and over again the teachers and I placed ourselves and our students in the position of giving voice to inchoate thoughts about the materials with which we were working. We talked—we thought out loud, we argued, we agreed. We sat quietly and wrote about what seemed important to us. We made diagrams trying to show how something had happened. In these ways we kept shaping and reshaping our ideas. Our goal was to "move beyond the bonds of human sense," as Scottish child psychologist Margaret Donaldson (1978) puts it. Moving beyond sense seems counterintuitive, but what Donaldson means is moving beyond the connotation of "sense" as "nerves and brain receiving and reacting to stimuli" to develop higher intellectual skills of thinking and control over thinking. Making meaning about the immediacies of living in the world requires the flexibility of thinking that is characteristic of successful scientists. We want to develop this kind of flexibility while children are in elementary school, so that when they move on to secondary school, where science is more highly abstracted, they can make better use of their intellectual powers to think about scientific explanations and evidence.

Children gain awareness of their thinking and begin to control it when teachers ask them to communicate their ideas. Here are some examples of teachers asking children to say what they think:

Teacher: What did you notice when you rubbed a spoon on the carpet?

First grader: When you rub hard, it got real hot. When you didn't rub so hard, not so hot.

Teacher: Why do you think the spoon wasn't so hot?

First grader: Maybe the spoon is made out of something different than the hand.

Second-grader: When we flicked the marble, we gave it a push. Each [other marble] went off to the side.

Teacher: Why do you think the marbles went off to the side?

Second grader: 'Cause the force; one marble hit the other. If the marble is pushed crooked, the other marble goes off the track.

Teacher: What are different ways of starting and stopping movement on the playground?

Fourth grader: When I jump up to reach the bar, I feel my legs are pushing me up.

Fourth grader: My feet are pushing and my hands are pulling. When you drop down, it's just gravity.

Fifth grader: When you're running and you stop quickly, your feet slide. Your feet slip. There is friction with the ground.

In these instances the teacher is "prising thought out of its primitive unconscious embeddedness" by asking questions such as "Why do you think ___?" and "What are the different ways of ___?"

We have found that children need a great deal of time and space to create rich, detailed explanations of the natural world. In the sixties, Elementary Science Study Director David Hawkins (1965) said much the same thing.

> When learning is at the most fundamental level, as it is [in children's exploratory work with pendulums] with all the abstractions of Newtonian mechanics just around the corner, don't rush! When the mind is evolving the abstractions which will lead to physical comprehension, all of us must cross the line between ignorance and insight many times before we truly understand.

Dutch science educator Jos Elstgeest (1985a, 1985b) also stressed the value of children's initially spending a lot of time observing the properties of whatever materials are under study, in as many ways as are possible in the context of the classroom and the environs of the school.

Teachers, too, need a great deal of time and space to learn how to sustain inquiry science and to guide children in their thinking. In the words of the National Research Council (1996), "When teachers have the time and opportunity to describe their own views about learning and teaching, to conduct research on their own teaching, and to compare, contrast, and revise their views, they come to understand the nature of exemplary science teaching."

From Hypotheses and Questions to Fair Testing

Albert Einstein identified the first aim of science as the formation of questions. Investigation questions are closely linked to hypotheses, because inevitably the questions contain ideas that can be proved or disproved in the investigation. Questions and hypotheses are two sides of the same coin. We found that once you get the knack of identifying appropriate topics, gathering materials, posing start-up exploration questions, and providing opportunities for students to share observations, then questions and hypotheses that lead to further work emerge, quite surprisingly, with ease. But, it takes a while to recognize them for what they are.

As the case studies in Chapters 5 through 8 show, each teacher was able to sustain science work that flowed out of the questions and hypotheses of the students. We found that it is possible to teach science in a way that is analogous to the writing process. In getting to this point we had to become accustomed to children working with the "stuff" of the natural world in short-term activities. We had to learn how to ask scientifically oriented, open-ended questions that result in action. We learned to pick up on children's hypotheses and questions and to move to new explorations based on their deepening understanding of the topic.

In the investigation stage, human sense gets its biggest stretch. This is as much the case for educators as it is for students, because trying to control variables is logical thinking at a high level. At the end of our work together, we were working on our understanding of fair testing and how to control variables. We learned to shape explorations and the investigations that grew out of them. Each teacher's story shows the ways investigation can vary.

I wish that we had more detail to report from the investigation phase, but because the teachers and I were so busy interacting with students every time we did it, our notes are practically nonexistent. As teachers we achieved a beginner's level in investigation. Students can go further, I think, when we as teachers learn more about fair testing and controlling variables. At the same time, my coauthors and I can celebrate many accomplishments. We learned to ask particular kinds of questions that lead to investigation, and we learned to listen, to generate children's ideas and questions, and to guide children toward the fair testing of their ideas. We accomplished a working understanding of how to organize science activity that leads to conceptual change. We hope others may gain from our experience and go further in the area of fair testing.

Conclusion

When Pat Pierce wrote her chapter, we thought that making the shift from exploration to investigation was the biggest challenge facing the teacher in doing inquiry science. But, as we grew more comfortable with making this transition, doing the investigation itself became a sticking point. Before these two enigmas emerged, we had struggled to elicit children's ideas and questions and figured out ways to do it. Our central focus kept changing. Together we shaped and reshaped what we were learning.

There is no question that teachers today feel pressured to cover far more over the course of the year than they have covered in the past. The listing of knowledge and skills in all of the subject areas in state and national standards, and the accompanying shift to local assessment of knowledge and skills, are part of a movement to hold teachers more accountable. It is perhaps only through a recognition of the interrelationships between science and other subjects that we can make a case for the amount of time required for inquiry science. Certainly inquiry science creates many opportunities to write, read, listen, speak, and use quantitative reasoning and knowledge, and many connections exist with history and such social sciences as economics and geography.

Elementary teachers are naturally resistant to the expectation of a high level of expertise in subjects other than English language arts and mathematics, perhaps especially in science. Yet science includes dynamic topics of high interest to many students, some of whom have special talents for science. Because of the many contributions of science to our lives, we need to cultivate this subject. Just as the ability to teach writing is enhanced by teachers' practicing writing, so too is the ability to teach inquiry science enhanced by teachers' experiencing it firsthand. Workshops, action-research projects, and study groups like ours provide a forum for doing inquiry science and for working out the challenges of putting it into practice.

In using an inquiry approach to learn about the natural world, we bring concrete materials, events, and living things into the schoolroom. This activates children's sense of wonder and lights a fire in their imaginations, bringing language to life in the schoolroom like nothing else can do. When children have firsthand experience doing explorations and investigations, they want to write and read about the topic. They want to discuss their ideas and listen to others' ideas. Math takes on a real purpose. The children's enthusiasm for learning accelerates.

Vygotsky (1978) reminds us of the value of play when he writes, "In play a child is always above his average age, above his daily behaviour, in play it as though he were a head taller than himself." In moving through several explorations to investigation, children stretch their imaginations in high-level thinking. In their play as young scientists, they walk a head taller than themselves.

References

American Association for the Advancement of Science. 1990. *Science for All Americans*. New York: Oxford University Press.

———. 1993. *Benchmarks for Scientific Literacy*. New York: Oxford University Press.

Atkin, J. Myron, and Robert Karplus. 1962. "Discovery or Invention?" *Science and Children* 45–51.

Atwell, Nancy. 1987. *In the Middle: Writing, Reading, and Learning with Adolescents*. Portsmouth, NH: Heinemann.

Boyd, William, and Wyatt Rawson. 1965. *The Story of New Education*. London: Heinemann.

Boyers, Peter. 1965. "Research Report." *New Education* 1 (November): 32–33.

British Association for the Advancement of Science. 1962. *The Place of Science in Primary Education*, ed. W. H. Perkins. London: The British Association for the Advancement of Science.

Bruffee, Kenneth A. 1992. "Collaborative Learning and the 'Conversation of Mankind.'" In *Collaborative Learning: A Sourcebook for Higher Education*, ed. Anne S. Goodsell. University Park, PA: National Center on Postsecondary Teaching.

Bruner, Jerome. 1960. *The Process of Education*. New York: Vintage Books.

Calkins, L. 1986. *The Art of Teaching Writing*. Portsmouth, NH: Heinemann.

Crossland, R. W. 1967. "Report of an Individual Study of the Nuffield Foundation Primary Science Project." Unpublished study lent to author by Wynne Harlen.

Department for Education and Employment. 1995. *The National Curriculum: Science*. London: HMSO.

Department of Education and Science and the Welsh Office. 1988. *Science for Ages 5 to 16: Proposals to the Secretary of State for Education and Science and the Secretary of State for Wales*. London: HMSO.

———. 1989. *Science in the National Curriculum*. London: HMSO.

———. 1991. *Science for Ages 5 to 16 (1991)*. London: HMSO.

Donaldson, Margaret. 1978. *Children's Minds*. New York: W. W. Norton.

Driver, Rosalind. 1983. *The Pupil as Scientist?* Milton Keynes, UK: The Open University Press.

Driver, Rosalind, Edith Guesne, and Andree Tiberghien. 1985. *Children's Ideas in Science*. Philadelphia: Open University Press.

Elbow, Peter. 1973. *Writing Without Teachers*. New York: Oxford University Press.

Elstgeest, Jos. 1985a. "Encounter, Interaction, Dialogue." In *Primary Science: Taking the Plunge*, ed. Wynne Harlen, 9–20. London: Heinemann.

———. 1985b. "The Right Question at the Right Time." In *Primary Science: Taking the Plunge*, ed. Wynne Harlen, 36–46. London: Heinemann.

Gagne, Robert Mills. 1977. *The Conditions of Learning*, 3d ed. New York: Holt, Rinehart and Winston.

Gardner, D. E. M. 1969. *Susan Isaacs*. London: Methuen.

Geertz, Clifford. 1973. *The Interpretation of Cultures*. New York: Basic Books.

Gega, Peter C. 1991. *How to Teach Elementary School Science*. New York: Macmillan.

Graves, Donald. 1983. *Writing: Teachers and Children at Work*. Portsmouth, NH: Heinemann.

Gunstone, Richard, and Michael Watts. 1985. "Force and Motion." In *Children's Ideas in Science*, ed. Rosalind Driver, Edith Guesne, and Andree Tiberghien, 85–104. Philadelphia: Open University Press.

Hall, Joanna S. 1993. "Experience, Experiment and Reason: English Primary Science 1959–1967." Ph.D. diss., University of Liverpool.

———. 1996. "John Dewey and Pragmatism in the Primary School: A Thing of the Past?" In *Curriculum Studies* 4 (November): 5–23.

Harlen, Wynne. Interview by Jody S. Hall, 13 May 1985.

———. 1985a. *Primary Science: Taking the Plunge*. London: Heinemann.

———. 1985b. *Teaching and Learning Primary Science*. London: Harper & Row.

———. 1992. *The Teaching of Science*. London: David Fulton.

———. 1993. *Teaching and Learning Primary Science*. Philadelphia: Paul Chapman.

———, ed. 1994. *Enhancing Quality in Assessment*. London: Paul Chapman.

Harlen, Wynne, and Sheila Jelly. 1990. *Developing Science in the Primary Classroom*. Portsmouth, NH: Heinemann.

Hawkins, David. 1965. "Messing About in Science." In *Children and Science* (February): 5–9.

Hewitt, Paul G. 1987. *Conceptual Physics: A High School Physics Program*. Reading, MA: Addison-Wesley.

Isaacs, Nathan. 1930. "Children's 'Why' Questions." In *Intellectual Growth in Young Children with an Appendix on Children's 'Why' Questions by Nathan Isaacs*, ed. Susan Isaacs, 291–349. London: Routledge and Kegan Paul.

———. 1958. *Early Scientific Trends in Children*. London: National Froebel Foundation.

———. 1961. *Early Scientific Trends in Children*, 2d ed. London: Ward Lock Educational Company.

Isaacs, Susan ed. 1930. *Intellectual Growth in Young Children, with an Appendix on Children's 'Why' Questions by Nathan Isaacs*. London: Routledge and Kegan Paul.

Jelly, Sheila. 1985. "Helping Children Raise Questions—and Answering Them." In *Primary Science: Taking the Plunge*, ed. Wynne Harlen, 47–57. London: Heinemann.

Karplus, Robert, and Herbert Thier. 1967. *A New Look at Elementary School Science*. Chicago: Rand McNally.

Kuhn, Thomas S. 1962. *The Structure of Scientific Revolutions*. Chicago: Chicago University.

Lampton, Christopher. 1991. *Bathtubs, Slides, Roller Coasters Rails: Simple Machines That Are Really Inclined Planes*. Brookfield: CT: Millbrook Press.

Massachusetts Department of Education. 1997. *Science and Technology Curriculum Frameworks: Owning the Questions Through Science and Technology*. Malden, MA: Massachusetts Department of Education.

Moffett, James. 1979. "Integrity in the Teaching of Writing." In *Phi Delta Kappan* 61: 276–79.

Munson, Howard R. 1988. *Science Experiences with Everyday Things*. Belmont, CA: Fearon.

National Research Council. 1996. *National Science Education Standards*. Washington, DC: National Academy Press.

Nuffield Foundation. 1967a. *Nuffield Junior Science: Teacher's Guide 1*. London: William Collins.

———. 1967b. *Nuffield Junior Science: Teacher's Guide 2*. London: William Collins.

Osborne, Roger. 1985. "Children's Own Concepts." In *Primary Science: Taking the Plunge*, ed. Wynne Harlen. 75–91. London: Heinemann.

Redman, Stewart, et al. 1968. "Young Children and Science: The Oxford Primary Science Project." *Trends in Education* 12: 17–25.

Schmidt, William. 1997. "TIMSS and Project 2061." *2061 Today* 7: 3–4.

Schools Council. 1967. *Science in the Primary School*. London: HMSO.

———. [1972] 1977. *With Objectives in Mind: Guide to Science 5–13*. London: Macdonald Educational.

———. 1974. *Minibeasts: Stages 1 and 2: A Unit for Teachers*. London: Macdonald Educational.

Simon, Brian. 1991. *Education and the Social Order 1940–1990*. London: Lawrence and Wishart.

Smith, Lydia Averell Hurd. 1976. *Activity and Experience: Sources of English Informal Education*. New York: Agathon Press.

Taylor, Barbara. 1991. *Get It in Gear: The Science of Movement*. New York: Random House.

VanCleave, Janice Pratt. 1991. *Physics for Every Kid: 101 Easy Experiments in Motion, Heat, Light, Machines, and Sound*. New York: Wiley.

Vygotsky, L. S. 1978. *Mind in Society: The Development of Higher Psychological*

Processes, ed. Michael Cole, Vera John-Steiner, Sylvia Scribner, and Ellen Souberman. Cambridge, MA: Harvard University.

Wastnedge, Ron. Interview by Jody S. Hall, 18 October 1990.

Weber, Lilian. 1968. "Nathan Isaacs: An American Appreciation." *The New Era* 49 (March): 69–74.

———. 1971. *The English Infant School and Informal Education.* Englewood Cliffs, NJ: Prentice-Hall.

Zubrowski, Bernie. 1991. *Raceways: Having Fun with Balls and Tracks.* New York: Beach Tree Books.